CHILDREN AT THE CENTER

Implementing
the
Multiage
Classroom

BRUCE A. MILLER

Published by

Northwest Regional

Educational Laboratory

Portland, Oregon

and the

ERIC Clearinghouse on

Educational Management

University of Oregon

Eugene

1994

Northwest Regional Educational Laboratory

ERIC®

ERIC Clearinghouse on Educational Management

Library of Congress Cataloging-in-Publication Data

Miller, Bruce A.
    Children at the center : implementing the multiage classroom / by
Bruce A. Miller.
        p.   cm.
    Includes bibliographical references (p.   ).
    ISBN 0-86552-130-1
    1. Nongraded schools--Northwest, Pacific--Case studies.
I. Northwest Regional Educational Laboratory. II. ERIC
Clearinghouse on Educational Management. III. Title.
LB1029.N6M49   1994
371.2'54--dc20   94-34054
                                                                        CIP

Design: LeeAnn August
Cover Photo: Kelly Fenley
Type: 12/13 Times
Printer: Cushing-Malloy, Inc., Ann Arbor, Michigan

Printed in the United States of America, 1994
Northwest Regional Educational Laboratory
 101 S.W. Main, Suite 500
 Portland, OR 97204
 Telephone: (503) 275-9549 Fax: (503) 275-9489

ERIC Clearinghouse on Educational Management
 University of Oregon
 1787 Agate Street
 Eugene, OR 97403-5207
 Telephone: (800) 438-8841 Fax: (503) 346-2334
ERIC/CEM Accession Number: EA 025 954

This publication was prepared in part with funding from the Office of Educational Research and Improvement, U.S. Department of Education, under contract no. OERI-RR 93002006 (ERIC/CEM). The opinions expressed in this report do not necessarily reflect the positions or policies of the Department of Education. No federal funds were used in the printing of this publication.

The University of Oregon is an equal opportunity, affirmative action institution committed to cultural diversity.

Preface

*T*his publication is the result of a cooperative effort of the Northwest Regional Educational Laboratory (NWREL) and the ERIC Clearinghouse on Educational Management.

NWREL's attention became focused on multiage, or multigrade, instruction in the mid-1980s as an effective, and in many cases necessary, approach for delivering education to students attending very small schools in rural, isolated communities. Initially, staff of the NWREL Rural Education Program concentrated on the role and concerns the classroom teacher faced with planning and carrying out instruction for children in two or more grade levels together in a single classroom.

Subsequently, as states such as Kentucky, Mississippi, and Oregon emphasized multiage organization in legislatively mandated educational reform initiatives, NWREL's focus broadened beyond small, rural schools. As Bruce Miller and his colleagues have continued their research and development work on multiage instruction over the past seven years, the importance of the school's organizational climate, parent and community involvement, and educational leadership and management has become increasingly clear.

This publication is based on the most recent research activities at NWREL to identify effective practices in terms of both implementation and what teachers do with children.

The ERIC Clearinghouse on Educational Management has long been committed to disseminating information useful for the operation and improvement of elementary and secondary schools. Thus the Clearinghouse staff relished this opportunity to cooperate with NWREL in publishing *Children at the Center* and in making it available to policy-makers, administrators, teachers, and others who are interested in multiage instruction.

Robert R. Rath
Executive Director
Northwest Regional Educational Laboratory

Philip K. Piele
Professor and Director
ERIC Clearinghouse on Educational Management

MISSION OF NWREL

The Northwest Regional Educational Laboratory (NWREL) provides leadership, expertise, and services that are based on research and development. NWREL services are designed to address systemic changes for the improvement of educational outcomes for children, youth, and adults in schools and communities throughout the region.

An independent, nonprofit institution established in 1966, NWREL is one of ten regional educational laboratories comprising a national network supported by the U.S. Department of Education, Office of Educational Research and Improvement (OERI). NWREL offices are located at 101 SW Main, Suite 500, Portland, Oregon 97204.

NWREL research, development, dissemination, training, and technical assistance activities are carried out in eleven programmatic units focusing on: (1) Child, Family, and Community; (2) Drug-Free Schools and Communities; (3) Education and Work; (4) Evaluation and Assessment; (5) Indian Education; (6) Literacy, Language, and Communication; (7) National Origin, Race, and Sex Equity; (8) Rural Education; (9) School, Community, and Professional Development; (10) Science and Mathematics Education; and (11) Technology.

MISSION OF ERIC
AND THE CLEARINGHOUSE

The Educational Resources Information Center (ERIC) is a national information system operated by the U.S. Department of Education. ERIC serves the educational community by disseminating research results and other resource information that can be used in developing more effective educational programs.

The ERIC Clearinghouse on Educational Management, one of several such units in the system, was established at the University of Oregon in 1966. The Clearinghouse and its companion units process research reports and journal articles for announcement in ERIC's index and abstract bulletins.

Research reports are announced in *Resources in Education* (*RIE*), available in many libraries and by subscription from the United States Government Printing Office, Washington, D.C. 20402-9371.

Most of the documents listed in *RIE* can be purchased through the ERIC Document Reproduction Service, operated by Cincinnati Bell Information Systems.

Journal articles are announced in *Current Index to Journals in Education. CIJE* is also available in many libraries and can be ordered from Oryx Press, 4041 North Central Avenue at Indian School, Suite 700, Phoenix, Arizona 85012. Semiannual cumulations can be ordered separately.

Besides processing documents and journal articles, the Clearinghouse prepares bibliographies, literature reviews, monographs, and other interpretive research studies on topics in its educational area.

Contents

List of Tables

List of Figures

Foreword

*T*here are times when I find my professional life as an editor and writer blending with my personal life as a husband and father. Editing this multiage guide for Bruce Miller has provided just such an opportunity.

As I edited, I peppered Bruce with questions based on my life as a parent of a five-year-old as well as on my work as an editor: How is it that teachers in a multiage setting can address the diverse needs of children at such a broad range of developmental levels? Aren't five-, six-, and seven year-olds going to be left behind in a classroom that includes six- to eight-year-olds? What additional training does a teacher need to effectively teach in a multiage environment? How will I know if my child is doing well? How do you teach math to a group that includes five-, six-, and seven-year-olds? How do you assess these kids? How does half-day kindergarten fit into a multiage environment?

Frequently, my questions were framed by my search for a kindergarten for my daughter, McKenzie, as much as by my desire for a quality multiage guide. Should I seek a multiage environment, or should I go with what I know best and place McKenzie in a more traditional school? My personal frame of reference was based on attending public schools that consisted of single-grade classrooms, teachers who dispensed information as if it was a rare gem, and students who passively absorbed the material—or didn't, depending on how well they fit the mold.

Throughout Oregon, public schools are being decimated by a voter-approved property tax limitation that has class sizes swelling, resources dwindling, and the number of school days declining. Despite these constraints, some schools — led by dynamic principals and staffed by innovative teachers like those in this guide — are meeting the needs of an increasingly diverse student population. Their schools are emerging as true learning centers that honor the individual styles of students, encourage the unique styles of teachers, and address the growing concerns of parents and others who care for children.

Parents are becoming increasingly vocal about their desires for educational quality. For example, about a year ago, my partner Sharon and I got involved with a group of parents concerned about equity, individual learning styles, alternative assessment, parental involvement, rising teacher-student ratios, and other school-related issues. Our early discussions have led to the creation of a parent cooperative school that will open its doors this fall in the Portland Public School system. Already, there is a waiting list to get in.

Multiage education is a critical part of the charter for the parent cooperative school we helped create. But writing a concept into a charter is a world away from understanding how multiage education works in practice.

As I continued to edit and talk with Bruce, my own walls about multiage education began crumbling. I listened to the stories that the teachers, administrators, and parents tell in this guide, and I realized that their journey was motivated by what is best for children. I also noticed that they didn't provide answers; they offered ideas. But they also walked their talk: Every day, these teachers and administrators modeled cooperative learning, applied learning, shared decision-making, and other values that they sought to instill in their students.

At the heart of it, that's what this guide is about: the ideas, concepts, values, and actions of educators, parents, and others intimately concerned about the children in their communities. As an editor, I hope you find it a good read. As an educator, I hope you find it useful in your school setting. And as a parent, I hope you find it as provocative and stimulating as I have.

Tony Kneidek
Editor
Northwest Regional
Educational Laboratory

Acknowledgments

I would like to acknowledge and pay special thanks to the many individuals and organizations who supported and helped this publication come to life. I especially want to recognize the dedication and hard work clearly evident among all the people I interviewed and observed during field-site visits. It is their commitment to children that inspired much of my efforts. The following provides a list of all those interviewed:

Lincoln Elementary School,
Corvallis, Oregon

Interviews conducted
September 1993

Elise Bradley	teacher, 1-3 blend
Karen Eason	teacher, 1-3 blend
Ellen Germaneri	teacher, special education K-5
Larry Harris	teacher, 1-3 blend
Dan Hays	principal
Linda Henselman	teacher, 1-2 blend
Brook Leaf	teacher, 1-3 blend
Mike Martin	music specialist
Jerri Otto	teacher, K-2 blend
Kay Reeve	art specialist, K-5
Lou Ann Tacchini	instructional assistant
Mary Williams	teacher, 3-5 blend

Overland Elementary School,
Burley, Idaho

Interviews conducted
September and October 1993

Mrs. Beabout	parent/secretary
Kevin Bushman	principal
Kayelle Bywater	teacher, first grade
Helen Craner	teacher, mathematics
Tera Craner	teacher, first grade
Lucia Gonzales	teacher, social studies
Dan McCarty	teacher, reading/writing
Samantha McElhinney	parent
Jana Rogers	resource room

Nilene Turner	teacher, science
Delia Valdez	former math teacher; principal (other school)
Kimberly Whitaker	teacher, reading

Concrete Elementary School, Concrete, Washington

Interviews conducted October 1993

Joan Berg and Judy Shepherd	instructional assistants
Dan Brauer	teacher, Chapter Lab 3-5 blend
Sherry Cowan	instructional aide
Barb Hawkings	teacher, 4-5
Lora Hein	teacher, 3-4 blend
Don Jeanroy	principal
Mardi Johnson	parent, volunteer
Peggy Kerschner	teacher, special education
Marilyn Land and Hallie Elms	team teachers, 1-2 blend
Meridith Loomis	teacher, 4-5 blend
Deborah Money	teacher, 4-5 blend
Janice Schmidt	instructional assistant, parent
Lynda Stout	school secretary, parent

Boise-Eliot Elementary School, Portland, Oregon

Interviews conducted November 1993

Alexis Aquino-Mackle	teacher, 1-2 blend
Betty Campbell	principal
Erin Cason	teacher, 4-5 blend
Anne Hasson	teacher, 4-5 blend
Robin Lindsley	teacher, 1-2 blend
Sharon Sheeley	teacher, 3-5 blend
Vicky Swartz	curriculum coordinator

I would also like to thank Northwest Regional Educational Laboratory and the ERIC Clearinghouse on Educational Management for the insight in recognizing the importance of multiage education and the financial support that made the research and publication possible. The Society for Developmental Education also contributed to this publication by facilitating the distribution and collection of a multiage survey.

Lastly, I would like to thank the many individuals who edited, reviewed, and, in general, encouraged me to keep writing: Jane Braunger, Jerry Schwab, Steven Nelson, K.C. Jones, Tony Kneidek, and Marian Grebanier.

Introduction

*T*eachers and administrators from country schools to urban classrooms are hungry for information on multiage education. I see it in the numerous calls I receive as a rural education specialist at the Northwest Regional Educational Laboratory in Portland, Oregon.

These requests come on the heels of numerous research reports emphasizing whole language, cooperative learning, heterogeneous grouping, and developmentally appropriate practice, all of which have implications for multiage learning environments. Moreover, the requests coincide with legislatively mandated educational reform initiatives in Kentucky, Oregon, and Mississippi that also emphasize multiage organization (Lodish 1992). This legislative action has caused teachers, administrators, and parents to ask whether this is simply another educational trend or a lasting educational reform. Despite such concerns, educators throughout the nation are implementing multiage classrooms and schools with insufficient forethought, planning, and participation of key stakeholders. I can think of no better way to destroy a potentially sound educational practice.

Unfortunately, promising practices and innovations are often implemented for the wrong reasons or with little understanding of key factors such as teacher readiness, staff ownership, parental involvement, and collaborative planning. Each of those issues must be considered if the change effort is to have a positive and lasting effect on students and teachers.

This need for caution seems obvious but is often overlooked by well-intentioned administrators who fail to understand how unsettling change may be for teachers who have little or no control over it. In that regard, implementing multiage instructional practices raises important questions that should be asked and understood before the journey begins:

1. Why would a school staff implement a multiage program, especially when evidence from the field suggests multiage classrooms, at least initially, are more work?

2. What roles should teachers play in planning and implementation, and what knowledge do they need to effectively participate?

3. What type of school or organizational climate is likely to facilitate successful multiage implementation?

4. How should parents and the community be involved in deciding, planning, and implementing the change effort?

5. What does leadership look like in successful multiage implementation?

6. Are there factors associated with implementation of successful multiage programs that can be generalized to other settings?

These six questions provide the framework for this implementation guide. The answers to these questions are complex and can be found in the ideas, stories, and experiences of educators who have struggled to implement multiage practices, as well as among the researchers who have studied the multiage concept for years.

There is frequent confusion around the meaning of *multiage* among both practitioners and researchers. Such terms as *nongraded, ungraded, multigrade, vertical grouping, blends,* and *multiage* are being used, in many cases, interchangeably (Katz 1988, Miller 1989).

Such semantic confusion creates misunderstandings that may damage prospects for successful implementation. For this guide, I use *multiage* to mean two or more grade levels that have been intentionally placed together to improve learning. The child's developmental needs, regardless of grade-level curriculum or administrative placement, stand out as a key defining characteristic of the multiage concept. Ideally, there is a blurring of grade- and age-level distinctions as students blend into a caring community of learners.

The educators interviewed for this guide aspire to this ideal. I hope you find their experiences and ideas enlightening and meaningful. Above all, I hope you find this guide useful as you embark on your journey toward a multiage classroom or school.

Collecting Information
From the Field

*A*n illustration of the damaging effects of blindly hopping on the bandwagon—and a key reason for writing this multiage implementation guide—can be seen in the experiences of a teacher in an urban school system in the Midwest.

A Veteran Teacher's Story

Sarah has been teaching elementary school for thirteen years. A year and a half ago her school became one of eight pilot sites in her district to implement multiage organization and instruction. When school started in the fall, she found herself in a classroom with first- through fourth-grade students. In addition, test scores were used to place a representative academic range of students in Sarah's class. She ended up with ten boys and four girls. Sarah mentioned that this imbalance of boys and the placement of several students with behavior problems made the implementation of a multiage classroom especially difficult.

Sarah had received two half-day training sessions on whole language in preparation for implementing the new multiage program. Not surprisingly, Sarah said there was not much in the training for teaching in a multiage classroom. When she was interviewed shortly after school started, she spoke like a first-year teacher, full of anxiety and concern about her students. In describing the planning and implementation process that occurred in her district, her anxiety appeared understandable.

A new superintendent had been hired with an agenda for change. Within his first year, he had mandated multiage organization and computer-assisted learning. Sarah indicated she knew very little about multiage teaching or computer-assisted learning. In addition, the district allocated $2,000 per pilot classroom for materials. However, the money only became available in the fall, so teachers did not have materials when school began. To complicate matters, the school year began with a new principal, who, like Sarah, found herself thrust into the middle of mandated change.

Teachers in Sarah's school were all assigned to self-contained classrooms with a student age span of four years (that is, grades 1 through 4). Sarah mentioned that teachers did not talk about their successes or problems, nor did they conduct staff meetings where multiage practices were discussed. By Sarah's account, collegial-planning and staff-development structures that would allow teachers time to share their successes and struggles were nonexistent. Sarah, like her colleagues, was expected to implement the change alone.

Sarah also said that teachers were not involved in the decision to implement multiage classrooms. The plan was developed at the central office, with program success measured by standardized test scores. This created intense pressure for teachers. To complicate matters, Sarah said the computer-based learning program created additional tension. Evidently, the district contracted with a California company that offered a program in reading and math that guaranteed academic growth provided certain standards were met. One standard created special problems for Sarah: Students were required to be at a terminal for thirty minutes a day. If students missed the regularly scheduled computer time, Sarah and other teachers were required to schedule a makeup time to validate the agreement with the California company.

Five months after initially interviewing Sarah, problems remained at her school. Teachers had gone on strike and the pilot project emerged as an issue. Sarah felt she was getting a better handle on instruction, but she wondered what the long-term impact might be on students and teachers. In her building, only two teachers seemed to be comfortable with multiage classrooms. Several teachers had resigned. Sarah said she thought about resigning, but felt she could tough it out.

Sarah's story is all too common. She left the impression that there had been little or no analysis of such key factors as teacher readiness, staff ownership, parental involvement, and collaborative planning. And although Sarah had a small class size compared to national norms, she faced what many teachers would perceive as an extreme range of developmental levels without relevant training or assistance. In addition, it appears that minimal advance planning that involved Sarah and her colleagues took place. For example, while each pilot teacher received $2,000 to purchase multiage resources, there simply was not sufficient time to order materials and have them available for the start of school.

It also appears that Sarah and her colleagues had insufficient knowledge of multiage learning to use the money in the most effective manner. Moreover, the isolated manner in which teachers were expected to carry out a variety of reforms suggests that the changes were implemented without the most basic understanding of the change process.

Recent empirical studies and research reviews demonstrate that multiage organization produces beneficial results for students (Cotton 1993, Gutierrez and Slavin 1992, Anderson and Pavan 1993, and Miller 1989). In addition, the work of early childhood researchers such as Katz (1988) and learning psychologists such as Dweck (1986), Vygotsky

(1978), and Gardner (1983) provide practitioners with a powerful foundation and rationale for understanding and implementing multiage programs.

While there is a rich and solid research base for understanding and implementing multiage programs, practitioners often neglect to integrate it with other successful classroom practices. Worse yet, teachers can be overwhelmed by a plethora of change mandated by administrators unmindful of the impact that such reform efforts have on classroom teachers. Sarah's story is a good example of change imposed by a well-intentioned administrator who did not establish a process that involved staff and the community in the reform effort. Moreover, he neglected to provide the resources and training to adequately prepare teachers and increase the potential for success.

The research conducted for this document addresses this complex issue by presenting information collected from teachers, principals, and parents. Their experiences provided the grist for the broad implications and applications of multiage approaches presented in this guide. Moreover, to increase the usefulness of the research underlying this guide, nine separate sources of data were collected across a range of schools and communities (table 1). This strategy provided the opportunity to cross-check information and to note similarities and differences across data sets.

However, bear in mind that the purpose of the research underlying this publica-tion was to describe how successful multiage programs have been developed and implemented. Therefore, no effort was made to collect and analyze cognitive and affective outcome measures. Instead, multiple self-report strategies (surveys and interviews) were used to develop a rich descriptive picture of multiage practices and their perceived benefits in the four interview-site schools.

Surveys and Indepth Interviews

Open-ended survey questions were used to collect information in four areas: (1) reasons for implementing a multiage program, (2) factors contributing to program success, (3) problems or challenges faced, and (4) recommendations for those considering a multiage program.

Multiage teachers and principals, and a sample of instructional assistants and parents at four schools in three states, completed the surveys. In addition, surveys were given to participants attending a national conference on multiage instruction to obtain a broad cross-section of information from the United States and Canada. Finally, tape-recorded interviews were conducted with the principal and a representative sample of teachers (including curriculum specialists) and parents from the four interview-site schools (see Appendix A for a copy of the survey and interview instruments). Nearly all surveyed respondents were either planning to implement a multiage program or currently doing so, thus increasing the likelihood of obtaining well-informed contributions.

In fact, the four elementary schools chosen for onsite interviews were selected on the basis of their reputation for successfully implementing multiage organization and instruction and sustaining it for more than four years. Table 2 provides the demographic characteris-

tics for each school. Taken as a whole, these schools represent a cross-section of school types: large, small, rural, urban, small town, ethnically diverse, and poor. These schools also reflect a common desire to better serve the needs of students generally considered at risk for academic underachievement.[1]

Interview questions, in part, grew from an analysis of the survey data and were designed to gain an indepth understanding of how multiage practices became successfully institutionalized in each school. Beginning with a discussion of survey results, emergent themes and issues will be identified and then elaborated through an analysis of the interviews conducted at each school. Moreover, the ideas and words of parents, teachers, and principals will provide a rich and varied picture of these four schools as they have developed and sustained multiage programs. Finally, implications for practice will be discussed using the six questions presented above.

---

[1]Budgetary and time constraints limited the number of schools participating in the study. However, the survey data were used to broaden the information base beyond the four interview-site schools.

Table 1

Overview of the Sources of Data Used in Preparing This Report

Surveys	Interviews
National multiage conference (n = 202)	Lincoln Elementary (n = 13)
Lincoln Elementary (n = 16)	Overland Elementary (n = 13)
Overland Elementary (n = 9)	Boise-Eliot Elementary (n = 7)
Boise-Eliot Elementary (n = 4)	Concrete Elementary (n = 13)
Concrete Elementary (n = 10)	

Table 2

Demographic Characteristics of the Four Interview-Site Schools

School Name	Comm Type	District Size	School Size	No. of Teachers	No. of MA Classroms	Age/Grade Span	School Demographics	
Lincoln	Small university town	K-12 = 7,652	K-5 = 444	14	12	2, 3 & 4 age span	ethnic poverty	= 1<% = 45%
Overland	Rural	K-12 = 5,494	K-4 = 184	9	5	3 age span	ethnic poverty	= 76% = 96%
Boise-Elliot	Urban	K-12 = 54, 975	P,K = 768	45	6	2 age span	ethnic poverty	= 57% = 64%
Concrete	Isolated rural	K-12= 855	K-5= 405	17	14	2 & 3 age span	ethnic poverty	= <1% = 60%

Survey Results: Reasons for Implementing a Multiage Program

*S*urveys were analyzed thematically, noting how often a theme or topic was mentioned. Rank orders for the national and interview-site data sets were determined by selecting the ten most frequently mentioned themes. Since items were not ranked by qualitative criteria, the remaining themes were later included in the analysis of the interviews. This procedure ensured that potentially important concepts and ideas were not overlooked. For example, student placement was only mentioned once on the surveys but emerged as a frequent topic during teacher interviews.

Table 3 was constructed to delineate the various shadings of why respondents engaged in multiage instruction. The survey results indicate that practitioners paint a positive picture of the multiage classroom. For example, "benefits" emerged as a complex factor from both sets of survey data. For the national survey, "benefits children" was ranked number one; for the interview-site schools, it was ranked third.

In analyzing these data, the category "benefits children" was only marked as a response if it was explicitly stated. However, if a respondent mentioned a benefit such as "develops peer learn-ing," then a new category was created. From this perspective, nearly all responses suggested multiage practice benefits students.

Only two categories represent other reasons for implementation: "result of external forces" and "required condition of employment." The high priority ranking of "result of external forces" on the national sample may reflect where the survey was administered. The conference was in Kentucky, where multiage primary schools were legislatively mandated and have been implemented for more than two years. But mandates can be beneficial. For example, numerous respondents from Kentucky said that despite the mandate, they loved teaching in a multiage environment. However, as detailed later, mandates often are perceived as negatively affecting the change effort.

What emerges from the remaining categories reflects a strong and compelling belief that a multiage learning environment changes the way teachers view the learner and the curriculum. Respondents felt multiage "promotes a recognition of diversity that necessitates appropriate action" and "encourages natural development of each child." In other words,

Table 3

A Rank-Ordered Comparison of the Most Frequently Mentioned Reasons for Implementing a Multiage Program

Rank	National Survey (N=202)	Surveys from Interview Sites (N=39)
1	Benefits children	Promotes a recognition of diversity that necessitates appropriate action
2	Result of external forces such as state legislation or grant funding	Develops peer learning and positive peer relations
3	Encourages natural development of child (that is, encourages developmentally appropriate practices)	Benefits children
4	Increases continuity of instructional and interpersonal relations across school years for students, teachers, and parents	Increases continuity of instructional and interpersonal relations across school years for students, teachers, and parents
5	Facilitates flexible student pacing	Reduces evaluation and competitive pressures on children
6	Develops peer learning and positive peer relations	Encourages natural development of child (that is, encourages developmentally appropriate practices)
7	Wanted to do it, love it	Promotes positive professional relationships and interpersonal support
8	Required condition of employment	Required condition of employment
9	Encourages teachers to be more student centered	Encourages teachers to be more student centered
10	Promotes a recognition of diversity that necessitates appropriate action	Result of external forces such as state legislation or grant funding

it "encourages teachers to be more student centered."

Several other categories provide insight into how this change may occur. First, the multiage classroom helps develop "peer learning and positive peer relations." Moreover, by having students for more than one year, a "continuity of instruction and interpersonal relations" is created among all those involved: students, teachers, and parents.

As will be presented later, information from the interview data indicates that continuity across several school years was a compelling reason for considering multiage instruction.

Educators from the four interview sites mentioned that a reduction in "evaluation and competitive pressures on children" occurred in their schools. It appears that this relates to the increase in the category "peer learning and positive peer relations" because, under certain conditions, "evaluation and competitive pressures" negatively affect student learning and relations (Nicholls 1989). Interestingly, these educators also said that teaching in a multiage environment "promotes positive professional relationships and interpersonal support." Care must be taken in how much weight to give this category. As we learned from Sarah's experience, multiage, in and of itself, does not promote improved relations or guarantee support. Other key factors must be present.

Factors of Successful Multiage Programs

Many subtle ideas and relationships emerged from analyzing survey responses to a question that asked about which factors contribute to successful multiage implementation. Table 4 provides insight into those factors mentioned most frequently. "Having support" was the most commonly noted factor, which suggests the high priority that should be given to developing support among parents, principals, and the central office.

However, the form of the support matters. The best support comes from parents who are "well-informed and actively involved," from a "flexible principal who understands the change effort," and from an "active school board and superintendent." Moreover, there are suggestions for how support is developed and maintained. Support is not a given.

"Cooperation and ongoing communication among all stakeholders" is critical and should include "ongoing staff development that focuses on the change effort and includes the whole staff working and learning together." In a related manner, the item "teaching teams who are given time for mutual planning and collaboration" was ranked as important. Teaching teams not only provide support but also peer learning opportunities. In the analysis of the interview data, the importance of collaboration among teachers directly relates to the success of the change effort, especially when teacher teams are encouraged and supported with common planning time and shared instructional space.

Flexibility also plays an important role. Having a "flexible principal," a "flexible and well-organized plan," and "flexible teachers" contribute to successful implementation. Finally, respondents believe teachers need to know how to use the "teaching strategies" and a "range of materials that help address classroom diversity." Taken as a whole, the information in table 4 suggests that implementation is likely to be successful if a

Table 4

A Rank-Ordered Comparison of the Most Frequently Mentioned Factors of Successful Multiage Programs

Rank	National Survey (N=202)	Surveys from Interview Sites (N=39)
1	Having supportive parents who have been well informed and actively involved	Having cooperation and ongoing communication among all stakeholders
2	Having a flexible principal who is supportive and understands the change effort	Using open-ended teaching strategies such as hands-on science and math, whole language, and cooperative learning to ensure student success
3	Providing ongoing staff development that focuses on the change effort and includes the whole staff working and learning together	Having supportive parents who have been well informed and actively involved
4	Having cooperation and ongoing communication among all stakeholders	Having an understanding and belief in multiage instruction as a tool for addressing and respecting the diversity of how children develop and learn
5	Having active school board and superintendent support	Providing ongoing staff development that focuses on the change effort and includes the whole staff working and learning together
6	Having a flexible and well-organized plan cooperatively developed well in advance of implementation	Having teaching teams situated in close proximity to one another and given time for mutual planning and collaboration
7	Using open-ended teaching strategies such as hands-on science and math, whole language, and cooperative learning to ensure student success	Having a flexible and well-organized plan cooperatively developed well in advance of implementation
8	Having teachers who are enthusiastic, flexible, and open to change	Having a flexible principal who is supportive and understands the change effort
9	Having teaching teams situated in close proximity to one another and given time for mutual planning and collaboration	Having teachers who are enthusiastic, flexible, and open to change
10	Having an understanding and belief in multiage instruction as a tool for addressing and respecting the diversity of how children develop and learn	Having a wide range of materials that help address classroom diversity

systemic approach is used to consider all stakeholders—parents, teachers, administrators, and students. The approach should seek to build their support through ongoing communication that develops understanding and cooperation.

Implementation Problems

What are the problems or challenges educators encounter prior to and during implementation of multiage learning? The national survey group represents a range of implementation stages, from those just beginning to think and plan to those with institutionalized programs. The interview-site group, on the other hand, has been involved in multiage processes for more than four years. Table 5 presents the results of a survey question designed to generate information on the challenges and problems faced by those involved in multiage implementation. For the national and interview-site groups, "developing support" ranked first and second, respectively. Building support clearly represents a primary concern and need. This emphasis on support is not surprising.

Like any improvement effort, whether it be a new program or a new building, without a well-developed support base or foundation, the new structure is likely to collapse.

The areas of "assessing program changes" and the "lack of time for collaborative team and/or staff planning" ranked in the top four. Respondents from

both data sets suggest that using standardized achievement measures to evaluate program success is problematic. In a related matter, respondents suggest that additional time be provided for planning and working together. For example, creating a more valid approach to assessment requires both time and expertise; developing expertise requires the time to engage in staff development.

There were also concerns that focused directly on the classroom. As one might expect from their stage of implementation, the interview-site respondents mentioned classroom-level themes more often than did the national survey respondents. For example, the interview-site group suggested the need for "having appropriate curriculum that addresses student diversity" and "placing students so there is a balance across a range of areas such as academics, behavior, and gender." On the other hand, national survey respondents more frequently cited issues relating to the initial stages of implementation, such as "support, financing, overcoming staff and community resistance," and "forcing multiage education through top-down mandates." Only the classroom-level topic of "letting go of traditional grade-level thinking and instruction" emerged as a priority issue by all respondents.

Recommendations

The recommendations presented in table 6 demonstrate a high level of compatibility with the information presented in

Table 5

A Rank-Ordered Comparison of the Most Frequently Mentioned Implementation Problems

Rank	National Survey (N=202)	Surveys from Interview Sites (N=39)
1	Developing support for the change effort with parents, teachers, and the principal	Having difficulty letting go of traditional grade-level thinking and instruction
2	Providing ongoing staff development	Developing support for the change effort with parents, teachers, and the principal
3	Assessing program changes with traditional measures such as standardized achievement tests	Lacking time for instructional and collaborative team and/or staff planning
4	Financing materials, instructional resources, staff development, and change-related costs	Assessing program changes with traditional measures such as standardized achievement tests
5	Lacking time for instructional and collaborative team and/or staff planning	Sustaining the multiage change effort through such activities as monitoring implementation, keeping abreast of new research, ensuring staff continuity, and ongoing refinement
6	Having difficulty letting go of traditional grade-level thinking and instruction	Placing students so there is a balance across a range of areas such as academics, behavior, and gender
7	Receiving school district support, especially in terms of knowing and valuing the change through both words and deeds	Having appropriate curriculum for addressing student diversity, including curriculum frameworks
8	Overcoming staff and community resistance	(All remaining items had a consensus of two or fewer)
9	Forcing multiage education through top-down mandates, especially when the developmental differences of staff members are not considered	
10	Sustaining the multiage change effort through such activities as monitoring implementation, keeping abreast of new research, ensuring staff members continuity, and ongoing refinement	

the previous tables. "Securing support" once again emerged as a dominant theme. Moreover, many of the topics delineated in the table reflect ways of developing support. For example, if efforts are made to "educate and involve parents" in the change effort, they are more likely to understand and feel a sense of ownership.

In a similar manner, if parents and staff members are allowed to "visit a variety of multiage schools" and "plan well ahead of implementation," their involvement is encouraged and their role as stakeholders is validated.

Many of these recommendations also indicate the kind of condition or climate most conducive to facilitating and sustaining change. For example, words such as "trust, shared understanding, providing choices," and "being flexible in working with staff" are behaviors that promote positive working relationships. When people feel supported, involved, and trusted, they are more likely to take the risks necessary in learning something new. In other words, people are more receptive to learning (for example, letting go of traditional grade-level thinking and instruction) when they feel supported and trusted. "Sharing successes and challenges" provides an opportunity for trust building.

However, as noted by both survey groups, "staff have to desire and own the change; it cannot be a forced mandate." When individuals are forced to make a change, they generally feel excluded from the decision-making pro-

cess and their attitude toward the change often turns to resistance. Survey results clearly suggest that securing a wide base of support and ensuring that the community and "all staff develop a shared understanding of the change effort" is vital to successful implementation.

Several other themes mentioned in table 6 are worth noting. Recognizing that change requires time and persistence and that stress and conflict are natural elements of the change process seems like good advice. Too often, in the face of change, there is a tendency to equate stress and anxiety with competence as educators. This is why "communicating among staff about reasons for multiage, sharing successes and challenges" is critically important. Moreover, the unsettling effect of change increases sensitivity to the changes children face every day as learners. When educators join their students and become learners, they also become better teachers. In the process, they also become "open to new ideas" and are more "willing to take risks and trust that children can learn."

Summary

A multiage survey was developed and administered to two sets of individuals. Results of the survey provide information to help guide those contemplating the implementation of multiage practices. The first sample consisted of individuals representing a diverse cross-section of teachers, parents, board members, administrators, and consultants at-

Table 6

A Rank-Ordered Comparison of the Most Frequently Mentioned Recommendations

Rank	National Survey (N=202)	Four Interview Sites (N=39)
1	Strive to learn and improve as a staff and individually, ensuring all staff members develop a shared understanding of the change effort	Secure support early on from the community, parents, administrators, and colleagues for the multiage effort
2	Plan well ahead of implementation (1-2 years), focusing on slow, incremental change that includes an analysis of the impact on all constituent groups	Build trust through communication among staff members by discussing beliefs, reasons for multiage, sharing successes and challenges
3	Build trust through communication among staff members by discussing beliefs, reasons for multiage, sharing successes and challenges	Strive to learn and improve as a staff and individually, ensuring all staff members develop a shared understanding of the change effort
4	Educate and involve parents so they understand and support the change	Plan well ahead of implementation (1-2 years), focusing on slow, incremental change that includes an analysis of the impact on all constituent groups
5	Visit a variety of multiage schools and ask questions of staff and students about the implementation process, materials, grouping, whole language, hands-on math and science	Educate and involve parents so they understand and support the change
6	Secure support early on from the community, parents, administrators, and colleagues for the multiage effort	Visit a variety of multiage schools and ask questions of staff and students about the implementation process, materials, grouping, whole language, hands-on math and science
7	Persist, give it time, and expect some stress and conflict as natural to change	Be flexible in working with staff, meeting student needs, and trying new ideas
8	Staff members have to desire and own the change; it cannot be a forced mandate	Be open to new ideas, take risks, and trust that children can learn
9	Be flexible in working with staff, meeting student needs, and trying new ideas	Build a foundation of whole language, hands-on math and science, authentic assessment, themes, and integrated curriculum
10	Provide choices for parents and teachers who cannot support the multiage change effort	Staff members have to desire and own the change; it cannot be a mandate

tending a national conference on multiage education. This group also provided a cross-section of implementation levels. Some were in the early stages of thinking and collecting information, whereas others had implemented multiage practices in their classrooms and schools.

The second set of surveys was drawn from educators and parents who have been involved in successful implementation for more than four years. Hence, they have weathered the early storms of implementation and controversy, emerging with viable programs. More important, their programs were implemented recently enough for them to recount their journeys.

How can the results of this survey help educators make informed decisions regarding the implementation of multiage practices, and what additional information would be beneficial? From a practical point of view, these data represent the collective experience of individuals who, for the most part, believe in and are committed to multiage organization and instruction. Taken as a whole, these are well-informed individuals. However, survey data only provide us with general themes or topics and can, at best, only identify key points to consider in developing a strategy for implementation. The interview data, presented in the second part of this guide, provide the rich detail necessary for constructing a roadmap for action.

Implications

First and foremost, ensure that your reasons for change reflect the needs and interests of the children you serve. Respondents were clear on this point: Their number one reason for implementing multiage practices was their belief that it would benefit children. Moreover, practitioners must know what practices will produce the benefit. Will the benefit accrue through simply putting various ages together in the same room? Or would it be better to have the same children over several years? Knowing and understanding why you are implementing multiage is critical to its success.

Second, build a solid base of support among key stakeholders: community and parents, teachers, and administrators. Engage these groups in analyzing and discussing the reasons for change: Is there research to support the desired direction? Are there resources to help answer questions? If possible, visit a variety of multiage schools. Ask questions of staff and students about the implementation process, materials, grouping, whole language, and hands-on math and science. If time and/or resources do not allow for personal visits, then reading case studies, making phone calls, and securing videotapes may be the next best option.

Third, build a climate throughout the school and community that is characterized by open communication and trust.

Include people in the process and take the time to explain the changes. In the community, this may mean providing opportunities for direct involvement in decision-making, community forums, and other strategies for parent education. In the school, this means learning together as a staff, where beliefs and practices are discussed and evaluated. Above all, create an environment where people feel safe taking the kinds of risks necessary to change classroom practice.

Finally, be realistic. Implementation requires planning, patience, time, and an understanding of the process of change. Both respondent groups placed a major emphasis on planning at least one to two years in advance of implementation. Moreover, research on successful innovation (Miles and Huberman 1980, Fullan 1993), indicates that successful change efforts take three years or longer to become part of the everyday realities of school life.

As realists, one must recognize that ultimately it is people who are being asked to change. As the survey data show, it is difficult for people to "let go of traditional grade-level thinking and instruction." After all, most parents, students, teachers, and administrators have spent their entire lives in graded learning institutions. Putting a multiage program in place is easy compared to changing the way people think, especially when curriculum and the textbook industry are dominated by graded materials. Moreover, individuals vary in how readily they embrace new ideas, strate-

gies, and practices. Again, drawing on the themes emerging from the surveys, educators must avoid top-down mandates, especially when the developmental differences of staff are not considered.

Interview Results

*R*esults from interviews conducted at the four multiage schools provide detailed information at the heart of why the schools, their communities, and staffs have been successful at multiage innovation and change. An analysis of the rationale underlying their actions and how they have sustained their efforts through conflict, budget cuts, and staff turnover will be presented. In addition, the patterns of action that unite these diverse schools and the qualities that give them their own unique identities will be described.

What Could Be So Compelling?

Why would a school staff want to implement a multiage program, especially when evidence from the field suggests multiage classrooms, at least initially, are more work? What could compel teachers to give up the relatively safe life as a single-grade teacher? Survey results suggest strong beliefs in the efficacy of a multiage organization. Respondents cited better continuity, more peer learning, and more positive peer relationships as reasons for implementing multiage. But for multiage organi-

zation to succeed, a series of questions must be addressed.

1. What roles should teachers play in planning and implementation, and what knowledge do they need for maximum effectiveness?

2. What type of school or organizational climate is likely to facilitate successful multiage implementation?

3. How should parents and the community be involved in deciding, planning, and implementing the change effort?

4. What does leadership look like in successful multiage implementation?

5. Are there implementation factors associated with successful multiage programs that can be generalized to other settings?

Each of the interview-site schools represents a unique context and set of circumstances around which the introduction and development of multiage organization and instruction emerged. To delineate these differences, interview results are presented by school. A comparative discussion of the interview sites is presented with an eye toward drawing out implications for those desiring to implement their own multiage program.

Several interview-site schools, notably Lincoln and Boise-Eliot, began their implementation of multiage as an outgrowth of developmentally appropriate practice (DAP), a concept gaining national prominence in the last decade through major research efforts in early childhood education and psychology. The following section presents a general overview of the concept of DAP and its implication for multiage organization and instruction.

The Conceptual Foundation: Developmentally Appropriate Practice

Developmentally appropriate practice (DAP) is not a set of clearly delineated educational strategies that teachers can use like a recipe to ensure student achievement. Instead, it is a research-based philosophy of how children develop and learn. Research from the fields of biology and psychology demonstrate that human development occurs in predictable and sequential stages, but with individual variation as to when a developmental stage is attained. For example, we can predict a timeframe for when children reach the developmental level where they learn to talk. Moreover, we can safely anticipate that all normally developing children learn to talk. Be-

cause there is variation and diversity within a developmental timeframe, we cannot predict the exact moment when a child will talk. Some children may learn to talk as early as nine months while others may begin at twenty-five months—all these ages fall within the broad range of normal.

Lowery (1993) provides a research-based overview of these two dimensions of development. In the field of biological science, evidence supporting developmental stages has been established by periodic increases in brain size and weight, cellular growth within the brain, electrical functioning within the brain, and head circumference.

From the field of psychology, evidence has been established surrounding three phenomena: the individual's capacity to deal with independent ideas and to relate them in increasing combinations in two- or three-year spurts from about the ages of three through seventeen; the individual's tendency to exhibit the same kinds of behaviors and view of the world as other individuals within two- to three-year ranges; and the individual's ability, upon growing older, to replace each view with a more sophisticated view which, in turn, is replaced.

Variability among individuals constitutes the area needing the greatest attention because schools too often underemphasize or neglect student developmental differences. This includes both the timeframe for a developmental stage (that is, the two- to three-year range) and those factors that mediate differences among learners, such as social backgrounds or dispositions toward learning. Educators have traditionally taken a normative view of development. For example, by the beginning of first grade all children should be ready to read; by the beginning of second grade, all children should be reading. The concept of the graded school, graded curriculum, and standard achievement tests all rest on this normative assumption.

The philosophy underlying DAP stresses the need for a balanced perspective on the whole child in all of his or her complexity. This means that educators need to be just as concerned with the child's social, psychological, and physical well-being as they are with academic performance.

Moreover, child-development researchers have looked closely at the social and environmental conditions that facilitate and inhibit the short- and long-term development of the child. For example, is there a relationship between how children learn to read and their attitude toward reading when they are older? The answer, unequivocally, is yes. Many children learn to read text but seldom read for pleasure when they are older.

Lillian Katz (1988), a respected authority on early childhood development and education, suggests that the primary concern of educators should be the types of learning experiences schools provide and how they relate to the development of the child over time:

The developmental question is not simply, "What can children do?" Nor is it "How do they learn?" Children always learn. Learning is a neutral term. Children learn undesirable as well as desirable things; to mistrust as well as to trust, to hurt as well as to help. The critical developmental question for educators is, "What should young children be doing that best serves their development in the long term?" (p. 34)

Although Katz's research focuses primarily on the early years, her conclusions have application for both older children and adults. What learners should be doing to best support their long-term development cannot be described precisely. Individuals and environments are too complex for such simplistic thinking. Researchers have nevertheless identified several broad learning principles associated with developmentally appropriate practice:

Learning naturally occurs in all human beings. Children do not need to be formally taught and motivated to learn. They are naturally inquisitive.

Learning is enhanced when individuals actively interact with their environment. This means learning through a variety of ways that engage all the senses: observation, trial and error, building, touching, talking, reflecting, and so forth. In opposition to this principle is the view of learners as passive receivers of information.

Learning is primarily a social process involving communication and contact. Individuals exist in the world with others. Even when alone, a person's thoughts and experiences, if they have language, are derived from other people. Language competence is strengthened when learners have the opportunity to engage in dialogue with others.

Learning is a process of continuously constructing meaning through interaction with the environment. Learners develop attitudes toward themselves, others, and learning based on the meaning they derive from their interactions with the environment (for example, setting, people, activities, and so forth). Thus, a learner's disposition toward school, teachers, peers, and so forth grows from the quality of this interaction.

Katz (1988) has identified four categories of learning: knowledge, skills, dispositions, and feelings. Table 7 presents the defining characteristics for each category along with their respective implication for learning.

All four categories are important in the development of the child. Traditionally, educators have placed greater emphasis on knowledge and skill acquisition at the expense of dispositions and feelings. Similarly, they have placed major emphasis on teacher-directed learning experiences, ability grouping, and other instructional practices that treat learners as passive receptors of information. These practices minimize peer interaction, especially across a diversity of learning levels and experiences. For example, students may learn to read or decode text by a direct instructional approach accompanied by drill and practice. At the same time, they may never develop a positive disposition toward reading. This is especially true of students who find themselves in the lowest reading groups throughout their elementary years. These practices often produce negative feelings toward self, learning, and school, especially among children considered at risk.

Table 7

Four Categories of Learning

Category	Defining Characteristics	Implication
Knowledge	Refers to what we learn from curriculum and store in our mind, such as information, ideas, stories, facts, concepts, schemes, songs, and names.	Children acquire knowledge through exploration, which can be helped when adults explain, describe, and apprise them of relevant information.
Skills	A unit of action or behavior that can easily be observed and described, and that occurs in a short timeframe, such as placing letters in a sequence.	Children acquire skills in many ways: through observation, imitation, trial and error; with guidance from adults, through instruction, directions, and drill and practice.
Dispositions	Refers to attitudes or habits of mind that characterize the ways individuals respond to different types of situations. These include dispositions such as generosity, curiosity, resourcefulness, involvement, and hostility.	Dispositions grow from the diversity of opportunities provided for demonstrating the disposition, and from the confirmation of their value by others in the learning environment (for example, helpfulness, independence, inquisitiveness, and so forth).
Feelings	Subjective emotional or affective states such as anger or a feeling of belonging, self-confidence, and acceptance.	Feelings develop over time from the types of interactions children have with their environment. For example, children develop feelings of belonging in learning climates with norms of cooperation and inclusiveness.

Lincoln Elementary School

Lincoln is a K-5 elementary school located in the small university town of Corvallis, Oregon. Another college campus, Western Oregon State Teachers College, is located nearby in Monmouth. Both campuses provide a wealth of staff-development opportunities for veteran teachers as well as a steady source of student teachers and teachers seeking employment.

Located along a busy highway in a semi-industrial working-class neighborhood on the south side of Corvallis, Lincoln Elementary School is a sprawling, old building consisting of long, wide halls, narrow connecting corridors, and a patchwork of portable and permanent classrooms in a maze-like setting. In some cases, it is necessary to pass through one classroom to reach another. The building needs repairs and, some would argue, total renovation. However, the condition of the building was seldom mentioned during numerous interviews and discussions with staff and parents. Everyone seemed intently focused on meeting the needs of children, a large percentage of whom are considered at-risk.

Lincoln represented a highly energized learning environment. Student work hung in hallways, on classroom walls, and from ceilings throughout the school. Everywhere, children worked and interacted together. Nearly every area of the school was organized to facilitate peer affiliation and support. In some rooms, students read and studied on well-worn couches. In the primary classrooms, students worked alone and together on the carpeted floors. A group of kindergarten through second-grade students sat in a circle while a guinea pig walked from one child to another. Students talked excitedly about the next moves of the animal.

Mixed-aged groups of children, whether gathering around a teacher for discussion or focusing intently at a writing center, were the norm. For the 1993-94 school year, nearly every teacher chose to have a three-age (or three-grade) classroom span. During interviews, teachers indicated that a wide age span made them more sensitive and responsive to the diverse needs of students. In some ways, teachers were consciously unlearning much of what they had been taught and come to believe were inviolable educational practices. In general, they found the sorting of children by grade and ability to be detrimental to children, especially with the at-risk population they served.

Many classrooms have been modified with wide door openings between adjacent rooms. For example, door openings connected intermediate classrooms (grades 3-5), thus facilitating the movement of both students and teachers between instructional areas. Since the inception of the multiage program in 1988, the staff at Lincoln—as well as community members—have continuously broadened their efforts to focus energy, time, and resources to meet the needs of children. Analysis of interview data will focus on this evolving journey through the eyes of the teachers, the principal, and parents who collaborated in bringing to life their beliefs and vision for children and for learning in a multiage environment.

In the Beginning

When Dan Hays was hired as the principal of Lincoln School in 1988, it was indistinguishable from other elementary schools in the district except in one key area: the nature of the clientele. "When I arrived five years ago, the school was like others in Corvallis," he says. "It had a traditional approach to teaching and a traditional organizational structure for a K-5, 450-student school. What stood out was its lower socioeconomic base when compared to the other schools in Corvallis. And it had a reputation for having a considerable number of at-risk students, behavior problems, and other similar issues."

At the time, after completing a three-year examination of elementary education, a district study committee recommended that developmentally appropriate practice (DAP) be implemented. Each building principal was to provide inservice to staff on the concepts and strategies associated with DAP. "The ten schools were told that they could do this in a way of their own choosing consistent with the philosophy of DAP," Hays says. "The feeling was that areas around town were all different and each might choose a different way to go about it."

Hays took this advice to heart. A core group of staff members met with him and provided guidance regarding inservicing the staff on DAP. A consultant was hired from the local college. In addition, Hays developed several structures that would help build bridges between the school staff and the community. His first action was to create a principal's advisory organization. Unlike the Parent Teacher Organization (PTO) at the school, which attended to activities such as fundraisers and carnivals, the advisory group would focus on instruction and learning, especially as it related to DAP. At the same time, Hays initiated the formation of a similar group consisting of the school staff.

We try real hard to bring the parents along with us, and sometimes it's hard because you want to ask their input and yet we are firm in our beliefs. **Leaf**

The two groups maintained separate identities for several reasons. Hays honored teacher requests to meet initially without the direct involvement of parents. He also felt that the community would express their educational concerns more readily if teachers were not present.

Hays' long-term goal, however, was to get the two groups together to talk about their school. To achieve this, a relationship of trust and openness had to be built. Over the 1988-89 school year, each group met separately but regularly. Group members read and shared research, discussed their concerns, and expressed desires for a better learning environment for children. The principal, on his own initiative, informally shared information between the two groups.

Advisory group meetings focused on helping participants understand and talk about DAP. Often, research was simplified and summarized for use by the groups. "I have an appreciation for how difficult it is to take a book or pages and pages of written material and read and really understand it," Hays says. "One of my strategies was to provide excerpts and quotes to parents and staff so they

could look at the intent behind DAP and maybe understand and work with it."

Moreover, each group also identified what they perceived as successful and unsuccessful building-level practices. When the two groups had established a base of trust and openness, they shared their frustrations and concerns about schooling.

What did Hays do to develop trust and openness? "Nothing special," he says. "I sat in front of the group and we began a dialogue about our educational beliefs and values." As a result, Hays learned that both groups were disturbed about student behavior, the failure of children, and whether or not bright and able students were being adequately challenged. "I urged advisory members to throw out everything, as if they were starting all over," Hays says. And he asked them, "What kind of school would you build?"

I need to get parents to see that if a child is always at the bottom of the heap, then that's their view of themselves. They need to be on the top of the heap to understand that they're worthy of being on the top of the heap. **Hays**

"The notion of the old one-room school came back up," he says. "People were feeling that if kids felt more connected, more associated with each other and the school, that perhaps attitudes and behaviors would improve." In other words, if staff created a family-like atmosphere, students might respond more positively to school and each other, thereby improving student learning.

By the end of the 1988-89 school year, the two groups decided they would become a single organization in the fall of the next school year. In addition, there was consensus regarding the direction educational improvement would take. The core area of concern related to the transitory nature of the single-grade classroom and the impact that had on building positive relationships with students. Hays says:

> We saw at-risk kids whom teachers worked hard with to build a trust relationship. It would take them many months to get some connection, some bonding. By February or March, these kids would just begin to connect and build up some speed. Then the year would be over and the kid would be moved to the next class and the same thing would happen all over again. It was such a terrible waste. We concluded that if we have children stay with a teacher for two years, we could beat that problem a little bit.

Both groups also felt that mixed-age classes would provide older children with opportunities to take on responsibility, experience leadership roles, and gain self-esteem. Thus, parents, teachers, and the principal decided to pilot several multiage classrooms as a strategy to implement developmentally appropriate practice.

The eventual success of these pilot efforts can be traced to the establishment of a solid foundation upon which the change effort was built. First, through discussion, inservice, and application, stakeholders worked together to develop an understanding of DAP. During this time, participants developed a common belief about the efficacy of DAP and a shared language in which to communicate their experiences. The second structural piece was the development of positive working relationships characterized by trust and respect.

The staff and community of Lincoln Elementary School sought to balance a curriculum that traditionally had placed greater emphasis on knowledge and skills than on the development of positive dispositions and feelings. Through a process of self-study facilitated by the principal, they established developmentally appropriate educational practices and conditions designed to balance the learning environment with the whole child. Hays notes that during the first few years the staff focused on ameliorating student social and behavioral needs and then began placing greater emphasis on academics.

> We're in a lower socioeconomic climate, and the first and most troubling issue we were dealing with in our first two years was the social-behavioral side of this. Now we're moving to the academic. We're really beginning to sink our teeth into skill development and a stronger curriculum, and we're trying to develop some things that will help our

kids perform better wherever they find themselves.

In a similar manner, dispositions and feelings were the first area of emphasis in working with staff and community. Issues relating to curriculum and content in a DAP environment could not be adequately addressed until a climate could be created that supported and sustained a change effort, especially one requiring a radical rethinking of the way the school went about educating students. To cultivate such a climate, emphasis was placed on breaking down status barriers among people and recognizing the power inherent in shared responsibility.

"I'd answer the phone right there in front of my secretary because she was busy," he notes. "Similarly, if there was a mess on the floor, I might clean it up just as quickly as anybody else. And if there is a child in need crying, I might turn to the custodian and ask his help just as quickly as I would a counselor. I was showing respect for what they did and modeling for other people that we are all in this together, and we are going to share it together."

The Relational Foundation: Trust, Respect, and Sharing Power

In the beginning, teachers worked in isolation from their colleagues and from the community. Each grade, classroom, and teacher was separated by time, space, and curriculum. Professional relationships were coordinated around a schedule with little or no time for collaborative planning or decision-making. The physical design of the building limited teacher access to one another much like the cells in a honeycomb isolate the work of individual bees. The organization of curriculum into graded levels assured each teacher an assigned territory to monitor and protect.

To further consolidate teacher responsibility, students were divided by ability and assigned to classes: remedial, talented and gifted, behaviorally disturbed, and so forth. Moreover, within each classroom, teachers had nearly absolute authority to direct and control student learning. After nine months, most students moved on to the next grade or placement. The continuity from year to year was provided by informal discussion, testing, and permanent records. Teacher evaluation functioned to ensure the orderly execution of responsibilities within the existing organization.

In many ways, educators have traditionally given priority to maintaining an orderly environment. While administrators, teachers, and parents have been concerned with children's needs, they have not questioned traditional approaches to learning in a way that would change how the school system carried out its educational mission. In the Corvallis School District, the process of educational self-analysis began in earnest with the DAP study committee.

At Lincoln School, the DAP report questioned how current educational practices were meeting the developmental needs of children. Through the use of parent and teacher advisory groups, a process of self-study was initiated. This, in turn, created a context for developing positive working relationships among stakeholders. A full school year of meeting, analyzing, and assessing personal and organizational values and beliefs about the purposes of schooling provided an opportunity to build relationships characterized by trust and respect. Through this process, a vast majority of school staff members and community members developed a strong sense of ownership and support for the changes occurring at the school.

---

*I had a little boy say to me today, "You know, it's okay to make mistakes." And I said, "Yes!" That's what we want these kids to know. It's really powerful. **Reeve***

Mike Martin, a veteran teacher of twenty years, has been at Lincoln since DAP was first implemented. He reflects the feelings of many teachers and parents when he says he appreciates the way change occurred. He feels he has been part of the decision-making process, that his ideas have been sought, and his views valued. Martin reflects:

I like change when it's personal, when I can make the change, and when I choose to make it. I like it

when we get the opportunity to create ourselves. For example, when Dan opens us up with a vision of wanting students to be doing evaluation, doing synthesis, and creating things, he allows for staff to do that, too. In other words, we now have an open-ended, creative, and dynamic process for change.

LouAnn Tacchini, a parent who participated in the formation of the parent advisory group, says her direct involvement in the change process helped alleviate fears that her children were going to be DAP guinea pigs:

I came in with very big doubts and very big concerns as a parent. Ending up with two children in the middle of it is like, "Oh, my gosh, my kids are getting fixed!" It was really scary. I think everyone has to realize that this is scary for parents and it's also scary for teachers who have been teaching a different way for a long time. And, of course, it's changed because I've been a part of it and I've seen it working.

By moving slowly and involving staff and the public, Hays helped create the sense of a community working together in the best interest of children. Art teacher Kay Reeve felt the support she received from the entire staff increased her confidence. "It's a wonderful feeling," she says. "It makes you feel like you can do anything. And it takes away a lot of the fear."

Reeve says that the risks teachers were taking also provided positive models for children. "That's what we're trying to teach these kids," she says. "It's okay to fail. I had a little boy say to me today, 'You know, it's okay to make mistakes.' And I said, 'Yes!' That's what we want these kids to know. It's really powerful."

Her comment, "That's what we want these kids to know," reflects a powerful concept that underlies much of what occurs at Lincoln and much of what makes its change effort successful. The principal and staff model the values they desire to instill in students. This involves sharing responsibilities and opening up the decision-making process to include teachers, support staff, students, parents, and others in the community.

For example, each teacher was given a classroom budget of more than $650, which allowed them to make decisions based on knowledge of student needs. Jerri Otto, a K-2 teacher, points out the value she feels in controlling her classroom budget. "I can buy stuff," she says. "One of the first things I did was buy tables instead of having desks. So it's everything. If I want carpet, I have to pay for the carpet. But it lets me decide what is important that year in setting up an environment."

According to Hays, empowering people to collectively make decisions creates the basis for active participation in the change process. "Empowerment means allowing them the opportunity to participate in decision-making, in choosing what we are going to do," he says. "It doesn't mean that each one gets to dictate for him or herself, because I think

that would probably lead to chaos. But it does enable them, legitimizes their participation. . . . You have to empower the people to decide for themselves what they are going to do."

The Evolving Program: A Chronology of Change

From 1989 to 1994, Lincoln Elementary School focused attention and hard work on implementing developmentally appropriate practices throughout the school. A chronology of the various stages the change effort has taken will provide an overview of how DAP has evolved and where it appears to be heading.

From the outset, school staff and community representatives blazed a trail through uncharted territory. Since 1989 they have implemented site-based decision-making, a site council, DAP in a multiage environment, divergent teaching and curriculum strategies, multiple intelligence learning, and specialists in the regular classroom.

Since DAP was implemented five years ago, the Lincoln community has focused its efforts on meeting the needs of the whole child. This has been the guiding criteria for making all decisions within the school. Hays is philosophic when asked about the mission and vision of the school:

> I couldn't say with confidence where we're going. What we're trying to do is respond to the emerging pic-

ture, and we can't predict what that emerging picture is going to be. I have a real deep desire to have an environment where we can embrace children, come to know them as human beings, and nurture their growth and development as they move on toward their teen years. I'm driven by the concept of a principal who says, "Your role is to meet the needs of children wherever they are."

The 1988-89 school year: The foundation phase

In the first year, the school and community developed a positive relationship around the concept of DAP and its application to the students and adults at Lincoln. After careful study, parent and staff advisory groups decided to pilot several two-age/grade multiage classrooms. Stakeholders believed the multiage environment would provide more continuity in the lives of the at-risk children served by the school.

"The most central piece we saw was that teachers worked hard to build a trust relationship, to get some connection, some bonding," Hays says. "By February or March, [when students] would begin to connect, the year would be nearly over." Moreover, Hays adds, multiage classrooms would create opportunities for children to exercise leadership and helping behaviors. "In mixed classes, older children would get real experiences of responsibility and leadership and would help with self-esteem."

The 1989-90 school year: The pilot phase, year 1

Unlike combination classrooms, where each grade is taught separately, the multiage blended classrooms deliberately blur grade distinctions in favor of an emphasis on the notion of a family of learners. In other words, instruction is based on the developmental needs of students rather than grade or curriculum levels. Parents and teachers decided whether to have a straight-grade or a blended-age classroom. It was hoped that the blends would help answer two questions:

1. Does having the same students for more than one year facilitate the development of trust and bonding with the teacher and enhance learning from one year to the next?

2. Do blends provide the opportunity for responsibility and leadership that facilitates growth of student self-esteem?

Person after person told positive stories, hopeful stories, enthusiastic stories about what was happening with their children. **Hays**

By the end of the school year, Hays says, the blends appeared to improve student leadership, responsibility, and self-esteem for all ages. Children and families also seemed pleased that they would be returning to the same teachers. The real benefits of the continuity could not be assessed until the following year, when half the children would return to the same teachers.

The reforms at Lincoln also sparked dissension among parents; some claimed that Hays was trying to ruin the school. More than ninety people attended a meeting organized by the parent advisory group to discuss the program.

Hays was unsure of what to expect, but by the end of the meeting it was clear that the program had overwhelming parent support. "Person after person told positive stories, hopeful stories, enthusiastic stories about what was happening with their children," he says.

Because parents and staff played an active part in the decisions that led to the multiage program, a potentially explosive situation was disarmed and the program allowed to continue and evolve. Interestingly, this conflict solidified community and staff beliefs regarding the value of the program and the importance of its survival. "The salvation for all of us was the tremendous sense of camaraderie that developed among most of the people in this building," Hays says. "They were ready to fight to protect what they believed in, what they were working toward." However, there remained four teachers who did not share the same level of enthusiasm toward DAP and multiage organization as their colleagues. Eventually, each of them transfered to other schools.

The 1990-91 school year: The shakedown cruise

During this phase, parents and teachers reinforced their commitment to multiage classrooms and discontinued the practice of providing a single-grade class for each grade level. More than 50 percent of the teachers chose mixed-age classes.

I was trying to teach long-division to a child who was having difficulty. I just threw my arms up and said to the kid standing by me, "Work with her." Two minutes and the girl came back and said, "Gee, Mrs. Williams, this is easy." And I thought, you have to use the kids as resources. **Williams**

By the end of the second year of pilot testing, Hays says an "incredible amount of disruption and polarization had developed." While some teachers wanted to continue with multiage classrooms, others wanted to return to a straight grade. Nearly everyone interviewed describes this period as very stressful and full of conflict. A mixed-age primary-level teacher said the conflict sent a mixed message to the community that jeopardized the program's success.

As a result, an all-staff meeting was called, and Hays openly addressed the conflict in terms of the school's mission to be an open and caring community.

"There was such a hullabaloo not only internally but also externally. Factions developed all over the place," says Hays. "We had at that time developed as our mission that we are a caring, courageous community. We brought everybody together and said, 'This will not work. We care about people and what we are doing now is not caring'."

By the end of the meeting, four of fourteen teachers remained adamantly opposed to multiage organization. In the spring of that year, two of the teachers transferred to a school that shared their educational philosophy.

The 1991-92 school year: Full steam ahead

The staff decided to go all mixed-age except the five sections of kindergarten. Three compelling reasons drove the decision: the benefits for children, the power of a collaborative culture, and overwhelming parent support. Of the three reasons, it was the benefits to children that had the greatest impact on everyone. Hays says:

> I would get [a call] on an average about once a month from somebody in the neighborhood angry because some of our kids were fighting or doing something really abusive out in the neighborhood. That began to decrease dramatically and disappear within the first year of reorganization. Also, we had a lot of problems on our playground with second-graders taking on the first-graders,

fourth-graders taking on third-graders, and that disappeared right away in the first year. . . . The teachers saw a change to cooperation and interaction. Indeed, what the parents had envisioned was evolving— the old one-room school notion of kids helping each other.

When all classrooms except kindergarten sections became mixed-age, the school environment began changing quickly. Teachers who had formerly taught straight grades now found themselves facing different instructional issues. They became painfully aware of the diversity among children. With a change to a more collaborative climate and the expertise gained from the pilot phase, these teachers sought the help and support of their colleagues. Art teacher Kay Reeve, who visited all the classrooms, says changes were dramatic:

> Instead of sitting in their desks in little rows and listening to the teacher, I began to see children working here on tubes, building, counting; children over there working with paints and paper. Classrooms began to function in a different way, where the child became the center of what they learn each day. "What are your goals?" "How will you do this?" "What is your plan?" Instead of the teacher being the director of everything, the children became much more involved.

That spring, a third teacher transferred to another school, leaving only one of the original four dissenters at Lincoln.

The 1992-93 school year: Settling in

During this year, only two sections of kindergarten remained as straight grades. The rest of the school reorganized into various multiage configurations of two- and three-age blends. With the major conflicts surrounding implementation behind them, staff members settled into a year of refining existing changes. However, as their reputation spread, they found themselves deluged with visitors seeking answers about implementing multiage.

Ironically, as Hays points out, there are no answers except the ones a school and community uncover through self-study and careful analysis of what is best for their children. "I think people have to go through the process of self-analysis, self-development, and self-training until they are ready to have some success," Hays says. "They cannot do that overnight. It is not a quick fix. And, indeed, mixing ages is not the issue. The issue is developmentally appropriate practice."

Moreover, as the Lincoln parent advisory group reminded Hays, self-study needs to be ongoing. For example, staff members became increasingly absorbed in their unique teaching situations. In previous years, staff members had collectively struggled to implement DAP. Now, though, they found themselves working intently in age-level teams. As a result, a perception of fragmentation surfaced with the parent advisory group. Awareness of the concern began with the site council saying, "We're not to-gether right now. We are kind of fragmented and we are losing our focus and direction."

After careful reflection, Hays decided to bring everyone together and review their evolution as a community, focusing on the why and how of their progress. "I had them do this in small groups, identifying the problems we had four years ago, and recalling the solutions we chose to act upon to solve those problems," he says. "Then we discussed how that's all playing out today. This brought our focus back. We realized that our working so hard in the small teams had fragmented our sense of community."

The end result was an affirmation and celebration of what had been accomplished and the identification of their next steps as a team. These included a clear delineation of three levels of collaboration: small instructional teams (two or three staff), wing teams (six or eight staff), and the school team (all certificated and support staff). There was a clear recognition, Hays says, of the importance and value of each of the teams, and a commitment to maintaining their viability and function.

At the same time, a set of issues, organized into three general areas, was collectively developed to provide focus for the coming school year. First were those issues relating to developmentally appropriate practices such as teaming, multiage organization, integrative education, multiple intelligence (that is, learning styles), open-ended instruction, and assessment. The second cluster of issues related to developing student responsibility through problem solving. Finally, the team identified systemwide issues such as site-based council management, training new people, parent communication and involvement, balancing one's personal and professional lives, and networking and coordination with local colleges.

Most important, staff acted immediately to address concerns by brainstorming short- and long-term strategies. For example, they decided to change staff meeting formats to reflect the three levels of teaming and to form several committees to work on assessment and systemwide issues.

By the summer of 1992, the assessment committee had completed a model (figure 1) of assessment appropriate for Lincoln School. The model, in keeping with their philosophy of DAP, provides a clear picture of the child-centered nature of the changes that have taken place at their school. A key element was developing a reporting system for parents that would reflect the assessment model. As seen in the last box in figure 1, the staff chose an approach using multiple methods, with goal-setting as a driving strategy.

With the spring came a budget crunch: The school was forced to reduce its budget by more than 10 percent because of a voter-approved state property tax limitation. The site council and staff collaborated to ensure program priorities would be maintained, and teachers chose to increase their class loads to preserve the performing arts program. Mike Martin, the music and drama teacher, felt this decision portrayed the high level of commitment to students as well as the need for flexible blocks of time. "The whole faculty voted last year to actually eliminate four classroom teachers [positions], up their loads, and keep all the specialists," Martin says. "I mean, not many do that. I really feel good that we have that support. They also wanted flex time; they wanted us to have the time to have a script-writing group and to work with drama."

By the end of the year, the site council and staff had refocused their efforts as a team and set priorities for the coming school year. In addition, the last teacher who opposed multiage instruction transferred to another school.

The 1993-94 school year: Expanding the vision

In the five years since the introduction of DAP, teaching, instructional organization, and community relations have undergone major transformations. A comparison of a 1993-94 school map with those of previous years portrays a concrete picture of the changes that have taken place. Every class, except one section of kindergarten, is multiage. Ten classrooms are organized around a three-age/grade span, while three classrooms have a two-age/grade span. Connecting doorways have now been built between every adjoining multiage classroom, and teaching teams have become more for-

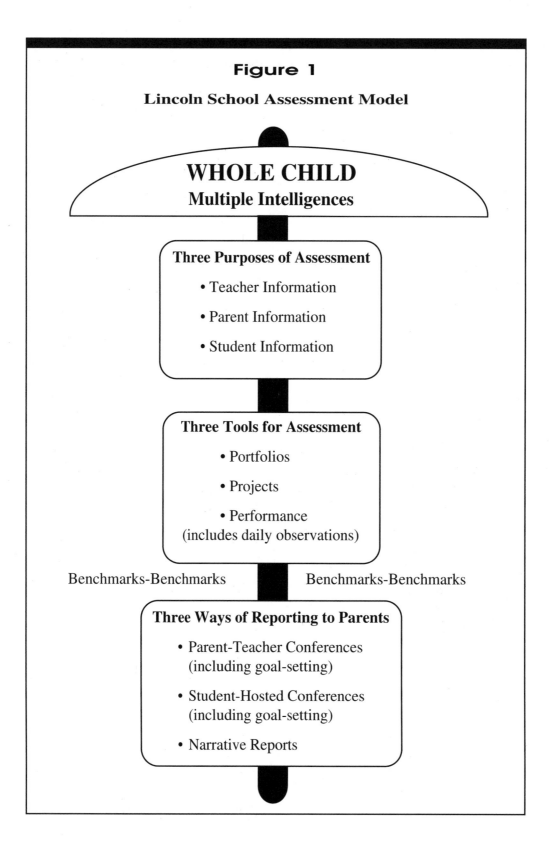

Figure 1

Lincoln School Assessment Model

WHOLE CHILD
Multiple Intelligences

Three Purposes of Assessment

• Teacher Information

• Parent Information

• Student Information

Three Tools for Assessment

• Portfolios

• Projects

• Performance
(includes daily observations)

Benchmarks-Benchmarks   Benchmarks-Benchmarks

Three Ways of Reporting to Parents

• Parent-Teacher Conferences
  (including goal-setting)

• Student-Hosted Conferences
  (including goal-setting)

• Narrative Reports

mal to include specialists and common planning time.

A new area has been designated as a community room, replete with couch, rocking chair, and decor with an inviting ambiance. A performing arts center concept has been introduced, and music, art, dance, and drama are centralized in adjoining classrooms. According to Hays, this was done to facilitate the integration of the arts into the curriculum. "We're moving to integrated instruction," he says. "We've given the art teacher a room and the music teacher a room next to the PE area. We're trying to develop a kind of performing arts center."

In addition, a former staff room has been transformed into a child care center, which currently serves about ten families. DAP, says Hays, must be extended to the early childhood years and address the transitions in children's lives. Hays says he is driven by a role to "meet the needs of children wherever they are." Clearly, one of these needs is preparing young children to enter the world of formal schooling. "We see ourselves getting more and more involved with early childhood education," Hays says. "We've talked to Head Start and we're going to get involved with Montessori and do some things that would actually help three- and four-year-olds get used to the school."

Hays also notes that test scores went up during the first several years of implementation, but have fallen recently. Although Hays understands their limitations, he also says, "I respect them as one way to look at our work." As a result, the staff will be "looking hard now at what we're doing instructionally and with our curriculum and asking ourselves, 'Are we allowing the behavioral and social side of things to dominate too much, at the expense of academics?' "

The Uncertainty of Change: Mapping Uncharted Territory

For most people, change is not easy. It means moving from the known and comfortable to the uncertain. Lincoln School staff and parents were no exception. When they began the move toward developmentally appropriate practice in a multiage setting, there were few schools in the state or in the nation that could serve as models or provide assistance. As noted earlier, some research was available and used by Hays to help create conceptual understanding. In addition, many teachers had developed expertise across a range of instructional approaches, such as Math Their Way, cooperative learning, whole language, and hands-on science activities. This expertise facilitated the curriculum changes required of a multiage classroom.

However, for the most part, their program evolved through a trial-and-error approach over four years. "What transpired here was four years in the making before we mixed classes," Hays says.

"And, admittedly, no models to go on, nobody there to help us. We were doing it pretty much on our own and in the search of what was right for kids."

You should be able to go into a classroom and ask a child, "Why are you doing this?" You should be able to ask a teacher, "Why is the class doing this?" And you should be able to ask the principal, "Why is all this going on?"
Eason

Interestingly, trial-and-error learning helped to create interdependence among a majority of staff members, a necessary condition of a collaborative work environment. Implementation had to be a team effort because the changes occurring in the school were significantly different than the ways most teachers had been trained or the ways they taught children.

Teachers found they needed each other for both emotional and curricular support. For example, Hays observed that when teachers moved into multiage classrooms, they faced not only more grade levels at one time, but different grade levels from what they had been teaching as single-grade teachers. This forced them to rely on colleagues with appropriate grade-level knowledge. Hays describes the changes he observed:

Another change I saw was that we had noticed how isolated all the dif-ferent teachers and specialists were. The mixed age drove them together because they had to collaborate in order to learn about a new age group that they hadn't worked with be-fore. The interactions increased dra-matically and I saw teachers going to each other for help and assistance and ideas.

Teachers and parents had to unlearn many sacred beliefs about educational practice as the school moved from teacher-centered, single-grade class-rooms to student-centered learning en-vironments characterized by a high level of student diversity. For example, a teacher of grades K, 1, and 2 found herself with a developmental span well beyond three grade levels.

Traditional ways of implementing cur-riculum, such as ability grouping and the direct teaching of convergent skill lessons to the whole class, were incom-patible with DAP and a multiage set-ting. As a result, teachers discovered many new challenges. To better under-stand the distinctive characteristics of the transition to a developmentally ap-propriate multiage classroom, teachers were asked to describe challenges and problems they encountered.

Making the Grade: Challenges in Becoming Multiage

The interview data provide snapshots of the terrain perceived to be difficult as the school traveled toward a developmentally appropriate learning environment. Seven general areas emerged from the data. Although these areas are all interrelated, they are presented separately for the purposes of discussion. One also needs to keep in mind that many of the challenges have no definitive solution. They require ongoing attention and a problem-solving orientation that works best when there is a collective effort among key stakeholders.

Relationships

All respondents mentioned that staff and community relationships had been of primary concern during all phases of planning and implementation. Especially problematic during initial stages of implementation were staff members who adamantly opposed the changes occurring in the school. They engaged in obstructive behaviors ranging from lobbying in the community to get rid of the principal to passively resisting efforts to collaborate with staff. By the fourth year of the program, these teachers had voluntarily transferred to other schools in the district.

Many of the problems associated with the resistant teachers appear to be related to an either/or way of thinking. In other words, some individuals believed that there was only one right way to teach. For some, the right way was multiage; for others, it was single grade. This attitude conveyed a divisive message to the community. "When the initial change was being made, some were teaching straight grades and some teaching mixed grades," says one parent. "There was a feeling of some doing it the right way while some were doing it the wrong way. Those kinds of divisions were an initial barrier or hardship."

Instead of saying "You've been doing it wrong all along," say, "Well, there's some different needs now that we need to change, to adapt to." **Leaf**

Another relationship issue surrounds the role of parents and community. Clearly, having parent support is critical if the program is going to succeed. One way to develop support is to actively involve parents in planning and decision-making. However, like teachers, parents are at many different levels of educational understanding and awareness. When seeking their input, how does one handle viewpoints that are diametrically opposed to the philosophy underlying the change being implemented in the school? Staff at Lincoln tended to deal with this problem through ongoing communication and staff-development opportunities for parents. In addition, the principal's willingness to actively listen to parents and share power by engaging them in decision-making proved to be effective in building a strong support base for changes in the school.

Adjusting to a wide age span

Learning to teach multiple ages together required rethinking how curriculum is implemented. Traditionally, teachers had viewed the needs of students through a sequenced and orderly curriculum framework dominated by convergent skill acquisition. In a multiage setting, teachers had to learn how to develop lessons that provided meaningful learning for a wide range of student ability. This meant providing divergent or open learning experiences. Fortunately, a majority of teachers had been trained in instructional approaches, such as process writing, cooperative groups, and project learning, that lent themselves to divergent or open types of lessons. Nevertheless, it was still difficult to let go of traditional grade-level ways of thinking about curriculum.

Comments from a parent and a teacher help illuminate this difficulty. "It's more of a looking at learning in a global manner," says LouAnn Tacchini, a parent with two children in the program. "It's taking a theme and making it work for kids over a broad range, not just teaching specific skills or facts about things that might be totally inappropriate for one age."

Linda Henselman, a primary-level teacher, says that lessons must be broad enough to reach all children. This entails providing children with choices, then focusing on specific skills as the need arises. "You've got to open up the kind of things that they do so it reaches every individual at his or her place, at his or her own level," she says. "You're teaching individually. When you interact with the children, it's according to what they're choosing—and you help them with their skills that way."

> *The children are so natural at teaching each other. And I'm trying to really emphasize in this room that we're all teachers, every one of us. And that they teach me all the time because I learn from them every day. They come up with incredible ideas and thoughts that I never had considered.* **Reeve**

Teachers also work to develop a community of learners where children feel a sense of responsibility toward their classmates. Reeve, the school art teacher, says peer helping is indispensable: "Children will sit at the table—two or three different ages—and they will listen to the directions and watch the demonstration," she says. "Some may not have understood a single thing, but they will watch the child near them. I've watched the children teaching each other and I think that's a powerful thing."

Some parents have raised concerns about the use of older students as tutors. One parent asked her son's teacher, "What are you doing to challenge my child?" Another parent was more direct when she said, "I don't want my child spending all of his time teaching kids who don't know as much." Although the issues implicit in these comments reflect perennial parent concerns for any type of classroom, they pose a much greater challenge in a multiage classroom. With a wide age span, it is particularly challenging to keep track of student progress. Teachers have to be especially attentive to each and every child.

Aware of the complexity of a wide age span, staff members have asked themselves what is the best configuration for multiage settings: two-age blends; three-age blends; K, 1, 2; 1, 2, 3; and so forth. The general consensus has been that a three-age span may best enable the teacher to see the diversity among students, thus requiring a change in instructional strategies. In addition, three ages also ensure greater carryover of students from one year to the next. Such continuity facilitates instruction because more than half of the students know the teacher and how the classroom operates. "Teachers are feeling that it is helping them be better teachers," Hays observes. "It also assures them that they'll have more carryover. We have such a high rate of kids moving in and out—that if they draw on a wider age span, then they'll be assuring themselves that at least half of their class has been there the year before."

Consistent with the school's student-centered philosophy, the decision to move from two to three ages is grounded in the nature of the student population. In other words, the continuity created in a three-age classroom provides more instructional stability for both the student and the teacher, thereby helping the teacher improve instruction. Hays is cognizant, however, of a potential problem: Student achievement could decline in an area if a teacher's skills are weak unless some compensating mechanism, such as team teaching, is put in place.

Implementation

Four general problem areas are grouped under implementation. Each area is presented as a question with a brief summary of how the problem was approached.

1. How do we apply the concept of DAP to adults?

Developmentally appropriate practice, according to Hays, applies to all levels of human activity, to adults as well as children. One of the first barriers that had to be overcome was a belief that being a teacher means you have the "right answers," that competent teachers do not fail or make mistakes. Karen Eason, a curriculum specialist, says that to survive a change effort, it is necessary to admit you don't know everything. "It's okay not to have the right answer, not to know what you are supposed to be doing," she says. "I think if you don't do that and you figure you have to know everything you'll never make it."

It's okay not to have the right answer, not to know what you are supposed to be doing. If you figure you have to know everything, you'll never make it. **Eason**

At Lincoln, Hays set a tone of trust and openness by modeling behaviors of acceptance and understanding toward the developmental differences within his staff. He consistently conveyed a belief in the staff's capacity to solve any instructional problems they encountered. Moreover, this was the same expectation he felt should be afforded students.

Ellen Germaneri, a special education teacher, describes the importance and the difficulty of dealing with developmental differences among staff members. In looking back, she voices some regret that they could not have been even more accommodating to resistant staff.

> Administration needs to be real aware of the levels of change that people go through. If you don't know what's in store, you have a lot of questions and a lot of doubt. If you're feeling you're being forced to make the change without having time to process and without having your questions answered or time to learn, there's going to be a lot of resistance.

2. How do we integrate specialists into the multiage classroom?

The reorganization into developmentally appropriate multiage classrooms allowed children to progress at a rate that was comfortable to them, thereby avoiding the stigma of not being at grade level. In addition, Germaneri adjusted individual educational plans (IEPs) to reflect classrom needs, then stopped pulling children out for instruction except on an occasional basis. Germaneri works collaboratively with the regular multiage teacher within the regular classroom. According to Germaneri:

> I might work one-on-one with a child or with a small group of children. I often float around and work with a lot of different children. This gives me the opportunity to see different ability levels in what the children are doing. It also gives me the opportunity to be more of a consultant and to give feedback for children who might need help.

Rather than fragmenting a child's learning experiences by pulling her out and labeling her, teachers work as a team to create the most appropriate learning environment for the child. This takes collaboration and time to plan.

3. How do we get the time it takes for planning and development work, especially common time among team members?

Time to plan individually as well as collaboratively is essential. By the third year of implementation, the staff worked out a formal schedule to provide common planning time for instructional teams. However, several people reported the schedule needed further refinement. In addition, the specialists for music, art, P.E., and special education said they needed to improve communication with regular teachers so they could improve support. The staff discussed this need and restructured staff meetings around team coordination.

4. How do we slow the pace of change, especially when we see so many ideas worth trying?

As the staff made more decisions about instruction and organization, they also became more energized and committed to the change effort. As a result, the program took on a momentum of its own. Hays found himself having to remind staff members to balance their professional and personal lives. The willingness of staff members to work hard speaks to their level of commitment to students. "I want to know all I can know about cooperative learning," says one teacher. "I want to know all I can know about multiple intelligences and the project approach and integration—all of those kinds of things—because I think it is all part of developmentally appropriate practice."

Slowing the pace of change may not be possible in any absolute sense, but steps can be taken to ensure people are not overwhelmed by the changes they have chosen to implement. A first step followed by several of the schools in this guide involved creating and protecting teacher time for individual and group planning and development work. Another step is to help staff set priorities so

energies can be used in the most efficient manner possible. For example, Lincoln staff members conducted periodic reviews of the goals and activities of their project, setting priorities they would emphasize for a given time. Finally, being vigilant to staff workload and providing resources to reduce extra demands on their time can also be effective.

Another teacher confided that the high level of motivation among staff members has "been really hard on teachers, the time they've put in just adjusting and learning. I mean, this building works on a lot of things at one time."

Assessment and accountability

Nearly every person interviewed voiced concerns about how to assess student learning in a developmentally appropriate multiage classroom. Valued outcomes such as leadership, responsibility, problem-solving, helping and caring about others, and positive dispositions toward learning cannot be measured by standard achievement tests. This is especially problematic because the public expects test scores to be an accurate measure of learning. Hays maintains that achievement measures are only a small part of what needs to happen in assessment to present a realistic picture of learning. As mentioned previously, the school has adopted an assessment model that relies heavily on more authentic measures, such as student portfolios, performance indicators, and projects.

Another issue raised during interviews relates to the quality of student outcomes. In a more traditional curriculum, student quality might be determined by the number correct on a worksheet or the percentage correct on an achievement measure. The Lincoln staff has been struggling with how to develop appropriate standards upon which to judge student growth.

Karen Eason, the curriculum specialist at Lincoln, believes this assessment issue is important because the more divergent, open-ended nature of curriculum in a multiage classroom requires a different approach. "When you're not taking the textbook and going from page 1 to page 210, then assessment takes on a totally different meaning," she says. "How do you know that kids are learning? How does a child know and how do you know when something is done and what quality it is?"

During the first few years of implementation, staff members also struggled with defining the appropriate behavior standards for their transformed learning environments. For example, one specialist indicated that students would walk to his class in a relaxed, talkative manner with little regard for the disruption they might be causing.

Staff chose to cope with behavior problems in ways that would build student responsibility. As a result, music, drama, and other forms of instruction were used to help students focus on appropriate forms of behavior. For example, Martin, the music teacher, worked with staff to develop songs about effective ways to communicate feelings. At assemblies, the entire school participated in singing songs and developing a sense of community. According to Martin, the students and staff learned a song called "Playground Rules," and staff and students sang and did a soft-shoe type of dance. "Everyone accepted and bought into a common language," he says. "We also did an 'I-message' song that was a heavy rocker number." These efforts paid off as the school principal and teachers saw a radical decline in behavior problems and an increase in positive student interactions.

Sustaining the program

Two issues have been grouped in this category. The first is how to keep the program vital while faced with budget cuts. In Oregon, schools have been faced with a major reduction in support because of voter approval of a property tax limitation. The most serious disruption is likely to occur in classrooms with younger children because they require more direct support until they learn to function independently. Lincoln classrooms also use high levels of hands-on, project-driven learning, which requires more planning and materials preparation. Additional financial cutbacks will be especially detrimental.

*With all of our changes—and it's been much more than mixed-age grouping—we always try to pull back and say, "Is this really best for the kids? Is this really meeting the needs of our learners?" We've been really good at pulling back and asking that. **Leaf***

The second concern reflects the need to balance professional demands with personal life. Nearly everyone interviewed described the implementation of DAP as a rewarding challenge requiring increased commitment and time. Several staff members mentioned that the principal continuously reminded everyone to keep their lives in balance and to avoid feeling they needed to do everything at once. He was also flexible about time, allowing staff to attend to personal matters as needed. "He focuses on building vision, building community, making sure people are taking care of themselves," one teacher says. "You've got two principals—there's Dan and there's the traditional, old-fashioned principal who watches the clock. No one watches the clock here. You're respected as a professional."

Learning to live with uncertainty

In general, the Lincoln School staff learned there are no permanent solutions or quick fixes in the effort to im-

prove student learning. The rate of change in today's world requires that school personnel and parents continuously examine and question their decisions and ideas in light of the changing needs of children. Brook Leaf, a primary-level teacher, says that assessing how an idea benefits kids is a mainstay of the decision-making process. "With all of our changes—and it's been much more than mixed-age grouping—we always try to pull back and say, 'Is this really best for the kids?' he says. 'Is this really meeting the needs of our learners?' We've been really good at pulling back and asking that."

*You have to trust intuitions, you have to trust children, you have to have the courage to operate in the black of night. No signposts, no road stripes. **Hays***

Hays believes this questioning approach is necessary to meet the diverse developmental needs of children. There simply are no clear roadmaps or prescriptions that make the educational enterprise predictable for any extended time. "We're talking about taking children in their many, many varied developmental stages and trying to bring them along," he says. "It is an incredibly complex task. You cannot simply label or categorize or sequence a series of steps that will accomplish that. You have to trust intuitions, you have to trust children, you have to have the courage to operate in the black of night. No signposts, no road stripes."

Enlarging the Rewards of Teaching

A major source of teacher commitment and satisfaction comes from directly experiencing success as a result of their own efforts (Firestone and Pennell 1993). If Lincoln teachers view their efforts as producing appreciable benefits to students and themselves, then it stands to reason that they would in turn feel more committed and energized in relation to their role as teachers. From what has been presented so far, this appears to be the case. Information elicited during interviews provides a wealth of supporting detail.

Table 8 presents the perceived benefits of multiage teaching for both teachers and students. Benefits are shown in descending order; topics most frequently mentioned are listed first. However, those topics are not necessarily significantly more important than topics further down the list. For example, the topic "intensifies the reward of teaching" was mentioned fewer than two times. This does not mean that few teachers are rewarded by seeing the success of their students in this program. On the contrary, the high level of teacher support and commitment to students and the program suggests this to be a highly valued area. In a similar manner, "increases flexibility of placement" is an integral part of the multiage classroom and would be considered by most teachers as invaluable.

You've really got to pay attention to how you're going to create an environment for the children where they can all feel good about themselves and they can still grow. I just think you have to be really willing and open to experimentation and trial-and-error and not be locked into "but I've done this before and I know it works." Just be brave enough to jump in. **Reeve**

The most frequently mentioned topics suggest valued consequences of DAP and the multiage classroom. As such, they constitute powerful reasons that drive the high level of teacher motivation and commitment emerging from interview data. For example, seeing students with increased levels of esteem ("build esteem"), valuing diversity ("value the diversity of people"), having a multiplicity of friends ("across-age friendships"), and helping one another and helping to create a caring atmosphere ("helping behaviors, cooperation") are highly prized outcomes of teacher effort as well as indicative of a quality program. Moreover, many of these outcomes appear reflective of the working environment of the staff and

Table 8

Perceived Benefits of Multiage Teaching for Teachers and Students (ranked from most frequently mentioned to least frequently mentioned)—Lincoln Elementary School

Benefits for Teachers	*Benefits for Students*
Builds continuity in relationships, learning, class management, and assessment	Builds esteem by providing opportunities for modeling and leadership among children
Helps the teacher provide a more developmentally appropriate environment	Helps children acknowledge and accept all developmental levels, personal differences, and value the diversity of people
Improves teaching by increasing sensitivity to diversity, puts student in the center of learning, and makes one more developmentally sensitive	Facilitates across-age friendships; promotes helping behaviors, cooperation, and cross-age/peer tutoring
Promotes collaboration and caring among staff	Promotes instructional variety: process writing, whole language, hands-on science and math, and so forth
Encourages instructional variety, thus making opportunities for expressing creativity and imaginative problem-solving	Allows the natural development of children by providing opportunities for natural groupings by age, maturity, interests, and so forth and a longer timeframe for growth
Promotes peer modeling of classroom routines and desirable behaviors	Reduces competitive and comparative/evaluative pressures
Topics Mentioned Less Than Twice	**Topics Mentioned Less Than Twice**
Diffuses negative attitudes among staff	Child becomes the center of learning rather than the curriculum
Increases flexibility of placement	Having the same teacher for more than one year facilitates an ongoing relationship with the teacher (that is, bonding)
Intensifies the rewards of teaching by allowing the teacher to directly observe the growth and progress of students over multiple years	Breaks down the status barriers of grade, performance, and ability
Helps to unify staff beliefs about learning	Promotes community, a sense of being a family of learners in a caring environment
Promotes the value and acceptance of diversity among colleagues	Reduces fear of middle school transition because students have already established friends in middle school

community as suggested in topics such as "promotes collaboration and caring among staff," and "helps to unify staff beliefs about learning."

Continuity across school years

Teaching children for more than one year has benefits for students, parents or other guardians, and teachers. For students, especially those at risk, having the same teacher for two or three years provides greater academic and social stability and eliminates the anxiety associated with yearly promotion or retention. Students also have increased opportunities to be leaders, which Hays says can play a critical role in a child's development. "When a child becomes eight in a six-seven-eight-year arrangement, we have to be cognizant of the fact that socially and experientially that child is the oldest and most experienced in that group," he says. "This carries certain rites of passage, if you will. If children are denied that [leadership] opportunity to be at that highest level, then I think you do something to their vision of themselves."

For parents or others raising children, developing a long-term supportive relationship with teachers improves communication and understanding. Building strong relationships with the parents of at-risk students is often difficult. But it is also critical because many of these parents have had poor relations with school.

*My child was extremely shy when he started school. Just being in the same setting and with the same teacher has been wonderful. He's actually in a classroom with K, 1, 2, 3, so he is now quite a bit older than some of the children in the classroom. And for him it's a real advantage. And he's opened up; he feels so self-confident. He can be a leader in the class. And his self-esteem is great. **Tacchini***

The benefits for teachers are equally significant. Returning students provide a steady source of mentors and models to socialize new students into the culture and routines of the classroom. Moreover, for the returning students, the teacher already has indepth knowledge of the child, which facilitates assessment and learning.

Having students for more than one year does have potential problems. What happens if the teacher and child do not get along? What happens if the teacher is weak in an academic area? These problems have been partially resolved by giving parents the choice of where to place their child and by using teaching teams.

In some cases, children have been directly involved in making the decision regarding their placement. For example, at the end of the fourth grade, one student requested to stay with the same fourth-grade teacher for another year. It turned out to be a wise decision. Says Williams:

> Last year I did a three-four blend with one fifth-grader. I had a child from my previous year who was a fourth-grader then who chose to stay with me. After really talking with him and telling him that it probably wasn't a good decision, he still decided to stay. It worked out to be a very good decision on the child's part.

This example also illustrates the flexibility of the multiage classroom and the influence teachers have learned to afford students. Teachers actively engage students in all phases of classroom life: goal setting, developing learning centers, teaching, and so forth. More important, this example illustrates the staff's child-centered philosophy. In most traditionally graded schools, this child's needs would have taken second seat to the graded curriculum—he would have been placed in the fifth grade.

DAP and student diversity

The graded school fosters the myth of homogeneity, a belief that all children in a given grade reflect the skills and abilities the curriculum ascribed to that particular grade level. Children not performing at grade level find themselves remediated or subtly classified as below standard. Students internalize these normative views of grade level and apply evaluative judgments to themselves when they do not measure up. Moreover, a status hierarchy emerges where the higher the grade, the greater the status. For example, being a sixth-grader is perceived as being better than being a fourth-grader.

In the multiage classrooms at Lincoln, students live in diverse environments consisting of multiple developmental levels. Students are expected to respect each other as individuals and to cooperate with one another. Competitive goal structures found in most single-grade classrooms have been replaced with cooperative goal structures and evaluation practices based on a student's social and academic growth over time. As a result, students become socialized as a community of learners and the hierarchy created by graded organization dissolves.

In a community of learners, children have manifold opportunities for mixing and matching with other students across a wide range of characteristics, among them interest, emotional maturity, athletic prowess, and age. The diverse population and the opportunity to be with the same teacher and students for multiple years increases the likelihood that the child's needs will be met. Because the entire school is multiage, the teacher also can place the child in other situations that may better meet the child's needs. Brook Leaf says that grade/age distinctions hardly exist. "We have a lot of three-grade and some two-grade classes, but when it comes right down to it, it doesn't really matter," he says.

"We're really allowing ourselves to place the kids where we feel their needs will be best met, regardless of their age and grade."

It has taken immense effort and hard work to transform Lincoln School into the learning environment described by interview respondents. However, the staff members maintain that the rewards outweigh any misgivings or trepidation they may have had during the early phases of implementation.

Overland Elementary School

Overland Elementary School is one of fifteen schools in the Cassia County School District. The district reflects a consolidation effort by the state that occurred in the mid-1960s. Overland Elementary is located in the county seat of Burley, a town of about 8,700 that serves a vast rural area in southeast Idaho. The district is 50 miles across at the widest point and averages about 7.6 people per square mile as compared to the statewide average of 12.57 (Oregon has 28.35 people per square mile).

Built in the early 1920s of stone blocks, the school now overlooks Overland Avenue, a busy arterial that connects the downtown area with the interstate freeway. A large storm fence protects children from the busy street, but does not diminish the constant din of cars and trucks. On two sides of the school, a grassy park-like area provides students with ample space to play; a playground with swings, slides, and a steel play structure occupies the remaining side of the building.

The 184-student school includes 12 instructional and support staff. Five subject-area learning centers, the special-education resource room, the principal's office, and the library are located on the first floor. The two first grades, preschool, community outreach, music, and lunchroom are located in the first-floor basement. The school is situated on the north side of Burley and serves what is considered the poorest section of town. The principal, Kevin Bushman, says many low-income migrant or Hispanic families live on the north side, where housing is affordable.

Railroad tracks separate the north side of town from the more affluent south side. This symbolism has not been lost on staff at Overland. As is discussed in the following sections, the low socio-economic status prevalent within the school's attendance area creates both benefits and problems for the school.

Bushman, trained as a kindergarten teacher, began teaching in the district in 1980. Six years later he was assigned principal of Overland. His leadership style reflects the tone and climate of the school. Bushman reflects:

> The first couple of years I spent getting to know the staff—a real small school with no turnover to speak of. This school is like a fam-

49

ily, and I tell people we fight and argue and make up. A lot of the decision-making and a lot of my job is done in a real pragmatic way. Whatever needs to be accomplished, we just get together and do it.

In many ways, this description reflects the informal nature of many rural schools. Bushman's understanding of and ability to operate in this informal setting may be an essential ingredient of program accomplishments.

Instructional Organization

The school program consists of grades 1 through 4; a preschool program is housed in the building, but does not participate in the regular school program. First-grade students are taught separately in self-contained classrooms. Grades 2 through 4 are organized into five multiage groups. Students first go to grade-level homerooms for fifteen minutes. During this time, teachers take attendance, complete housekeeping chores, and provide whatever support students may need. At 8:30 a.m., a fifty-five-minute rotation schedule begins. Monday through Thursday, each group rotates through five different learning centers: reading, writing lab, social studies, math, and science. Teachers serve as subject area specialists. The schedule changes on Friday, when first graders join the rotation. "Fine Arts Friday," as everyone calls it, consists of classes in PE, drama, music, learning games, and art. Staff initiated Fine Arts Friday to

enrich student learning opportunities beyond the core curriculum areas offered the other four days of the week.

First of all, don't be afraid of the drastic change. This was my personal fear. I liked a comfortable groove, and I thought, "This is too radical; it'll never work." But the more I got into it, the more I liked it. And my son liked it too. **Beabout**

By most standards, the Overland School clientele and program are unusual in this rather traditional rural community. Most visitors are surprised that this multiage program was developed and has remained viable for nearly four years, winning both praise from the governor of Idaho and a second cycle of funding as a Chapter 1 school-improvement project.

The Emerging Vision

Overland School serves the highest percentage of low-income students in the state. The school also serves the largest percentage of migrant students in the district. Seventy-four percent of the population is Hispanic. Standardized test scores are the lowest in the district, earning the school a reputation for being the worst in the county. The only advantage such a reputation has is that district officials are willing to give school personnel latitude in trying new approaches to learning. Through the coalescence of several key people and events, the school's staff was given an opportunity to test the limits of the district's support.

The 1989-90 school year: Developing the plan

In the fall of 1989, Bushman and the district Chapter 1 coordinator attended a conference on Chapter 1-sponsored, schoolwide improvement projects. Federal resources, channeled through the Idaho State Department of Education, were available for schools in which enrollment was predominantly Chapter 1. Funding was available in three-year cycles and could be used for any project that targeted improving student academic outcomes as measured by standard achievement tests. Unlike Chapter 1 achievement targets of the past, the new regulations placed major emphasis on higher order thinking and problem-solving.

Encouraged by information from the conference and district support, Bushman returned to Overland and "told the staff that we were being given the rare opportunity to do whatever we wanted in order to bring about the changes we need to make school work for our students."

The staff members began by assessing how well they were meeting the needs of students. Bushman points out:

> Staff agreed that they weren't doing
> a very good job of teaching students

for several reasons. For one, we weren't doing a very good job with reading. We also weren't doing much outside the state-mandated curriculum in math and science, and much of what we did was the result of following the "traditional/mythology" of education—"It has always been done this way."

The staff decided to apply for funding.

We can do anything we want. We're going to have the freedom to completely redo this whole thing—not based on educational tradition but on what's best for kids, what's best for learning, and what research says works.
Bushman

A major factor in the staff's decision was the need for change and the leadership of the school's "matriarch," Helen Craner. She had taught for more than thirty years, including twenty-one at Overland. Two years before the project started, she began serving as the school's Chapter 1 teacher. She is strong-willed and respected by staff for her dedication and commitment to children.

Craner was especially taken with the ideas presented by the principal and threw her active support into helping develop a school-improvement project. Craner's involvement sprang from frustration at seeing children continuously fail, drop out, or withdraw. She says:

I would go to the band concerts and hunt for my kids and they weren't in the band. I'd go to the ball games and hunt for my kids, and they weren't there. My vision was that at some point, if this program would work, then my kids would graduate from high school and my kids would be in band and my kids would be in athletics and my kids would be part of a group.

In many ways, Craner's views represent those of the entire staff and suggest the high level of need for change.

Because the staff was small and close-knit, decisions were made as a group. The first major task they faced was planning and developing an intervention program to be submitted in a proposal for funding. With inservice funds from the state, the staff began by envisioning what their school might look like if changes were made. Bushman told staff "to pretend we have the four walls, and that's it. We can do anything we want. We're going to have the freedom to completely redo this whole thing—not based on educational tradition but on what's best for kids, what's best for learning, and what research says works."

The state provided some initial staff development to help with planning. Hank Levin of Stanford University conducted a workshop on his accelerated schools model, which heavily influenced the Overland staff. "We decided that one of the keys would be an interactive, hands-on approach," says Bushman. "We also wanted to incorporate whole language, cooperative learning groups, and a col-

laborative use of staff and special services." As a result, a program was developed and christened with the acronym WINCH (Whole Language, Intensive Instruction, Nongraded, Cooperative/Collaborative Learning, Hands-on Instruction).

So let's treat kids as if they are talented and gifted. **Bushman**

A key principle of the program is the expectation that every child is talented and gifted. According to Bushman, when teachers begin to perceive students from this frame of reference, they "interact with them differently than if they see them as all remedial—so let's treat kids as if they are talented and gifted." With this idea in mind, three key dimensions of the school underwent major change: grade configurations, instructional delivery, and staff working relations. Table 9 presents a comparison of the school before and after plans were developed.

The school received notice of funding as a Chapter 1 improvement project in January 1990. This meant the entire staff was entitled to participate in any Chapter 1 staff development offered by the state, which increased funding, and, most important, waived many Chapter 1 guidelines. In their proposal, staff members said Chapter 1 students would show achievement gains of three NCEs (National Curve Equivalents). NCEs are scores that can be averaged and compared across grade levels and across

Table 9

A Comparison of Three Dimensions of Program Change

Dimension	Before Program Change	After Program Change
Grade Configuration	Students were sorted into first through fourth grades in self-contained classrooms.	Students are organized into multiage groups that rotate between five core learning centers: reading, writing lab, math, social studies, and science. Friday is reserved for fine arts.
Instructional Delivery	Students sat in rows, sequentially read textbooks, and completed workbooks and dittos. The learner was primarily passive, absorbing basic skills presented directly by the teacher.	Students interact in cooperative groups and are encouraged to help one another. Themes are chosen across the school. Teachers have become more facilitative of student activities and projects. An emphasis on skills development still predominates.
Teacher Relations	Teachers worked in isolation and rarely collaborated on projects. Talk and discussion occurred mostly in the staff lounge during lunch and in the hallways between class. Each teacher was responsible for a grade level and a specified curriculum.	Teachers have responsibility for a single subject they teach to all students. This creates common ground that unites the staff. Meetings for planning and development work occur frequently. Reporting to parents requires input from all the staff. Interpersonal communication and support are necessary for coordination of learning.

tests. Moderate gains would reflect five to ten NCEs.

With minimal outside help, the staff collaborated in developing schedules, choosing schoolwide themes, and preparing their classrooms for the start of school. When school was ready to open, teachers felt they simply needed an extra day to get physically situated. "We prepared before the start of school and then we felt there were still some things we needed to do," says math teacher Delia Valdez. Kevin Bushman went to the district and got approval to give us a day off to get ourselves physically situated. That was something that you don't see very often." When school began, the principal had randomly assigned students in grades 1 through 4 into seven groups.

The 1990-91 school year: The big surprise

With few models to follow and no opportunity to visit or talk with other multiage teachers, staff members launched into their first year of instruction with little premonition of how difficult the transition would be. As traditional teachers who were used to structuring learning around grade-level curriculum, they now found themselves in unfamiliar territory. Staff members described the first months of school as incredibly stressful and frustrating because their primary model of teaching (that is, direct instruction) and their emphasis on basic skills appeared out of place. The first refinement of the program was to eliminate first grade from the rotation. As Craner points out, teachers felt it "was too hard to challenge a fourth-grader and give the first-graders all the skills they need."

*I was really upset at the beginning. And other people were, too. There was a whole new thing, you have to go through the changing process. But once you get into it and you become comfortable with each other, it's not so bad any more. **Rogers***

Even with the elimination of one grade, staff remained apprehensive. Dan McCarty, a seasoned teacher, says:

The biggest difficulty that I had was that I didn't know how to start. I had second-, third-, and fourth-graders in the room at the same time. I wanted to meet all their needs. I knew I had fourth-graders beyond second-grade skills; I had third-graders in the middle. How do I prepare a lesson where I reach everyone?

During this critical phase of implementation, teachers felt especially vulnerable. They had their reputations as experienced, competent teachers to uphold. They had received a grant to produce a program that would demonstrate NCE gains on district standardized tests. And the central office was watching to see how things were going.

*Every school is different, every atmosphere, every faculty, and so you need to fit your program to your area, your students, and your staff. **H. Craner***

By the year's end, staff began to feel more confident. Student attendance increased, fighting and negative forms of behavior began to decrease, and students seemed truly motivated to learn. Moreover, staff gained sufficient experience to better define needs and make informed decisions about changes to the program. Bushman indicated there were seven key modifications the staff made during the year:

1. *The student placement method was changed to ensure a balance of gen-*

der and age. At the beginning of the year, Bushman randomly assigned students to groups. It became readily apparent that some groups were imbalanced in terms of gender and age.

2. *Textbooks were eliminated as a basis for structuring learning*. This required teachers to rethink how they planned and used activities, requiring more creativity and time. To use time more efficiently, staff decided to not switch their subject areas each semester as they had originally planned. This helped them develop greater familiarity with the content area. However, they still planned to switch at the year's end.

3. *Use of themes was strengthened in an effort to increase integration across content areas*. During the previous year, themes had been used on a superficial level, mainly around bulletin boards and in an occasional reference to the theme.

4. *Pullouts for the library and special programs were restructured to avoid disruptions during core instructional time*.

5. *Fine Arts Friday was created*. Teachers felt that the arts needed greater emphasis. They also wanted time when everyone could relax and just have fun. Students nicknamed this period "Fun Friday." First graders were included in the Friday rotation to help with the transition to the

multiage groups and to enhance the sense of community.

6. *Recess was eliminated to increase instructional time*. It was felt that the Friday activities would compensate.

7. *Student reporting format was completely revised*. Teachers felt the graded report card they had been using was useless in the new program. As a result, they created a reporting system based on specific skills with a place to indicate "mastered" and "still learning."

The 1991-92 school year: Settling in

After a demanding first year of implementation that saw teachers pushed to the edge of their knowledge—and, in some cases, to tears—staff embraced the second year with a renewed sense of energy and optimism. They found themselves featured as a showcase Chapter 1 improvement project that had both positive and negative results. On the positive side, they hosted visitors about every three weeks. In some cases these were individual teachers; in other cases, school teams. According to Bushman, the attention had two effects on the staff. First, staff members felt their efforts validated by the positive attention. Second, the presence of visitors tended to push the staff toward higher levels of improvement. In a similar fashion, teachers found themselves invited to present Program WINCH at conferences, sponsored by such organizations as the International Reading Associations and the Alaska Department of Education.

On the negative side, the positive publicity brought out jealousies within the school district, and the Overland staff was ostracized. One teacher describes being confronted in the produce section of the local market by a teacher from another building and being "read the riot act" about Project WINCH. Bushman hypothesizes that others in the district were viewing things in winner/loser terms, with an attitude that says, "Either Overland is doing it right and we are doing it wrong, or vice-versa." If Overland was doing it right, then other teachers in the district feared that their schools would have to become like Overland. The sense of being under siege only served to strengthen resolve among staff at Overland and brought them even closer together.

During this year, the Department of Education chose Overland to participate in a project to increase collaboration among special- and regular-program teachers. Staff members received training that helped them see the value of minimizing or eliminating pullout programs because they fragmented learning for at-risk students. Staff members also received training in cooperative learning that helped them better understand the potential of small-group learning.

Test scores at year's end showed students gaining, on average, nearly twelve NCE points on the annual achievement tests. This created some breathing room

for staff. "After we tested and we did score higher than expected, we all started to relax a little," Craner says. "We felt that we were accomplishing something."

The 1992-93 school year: Refinement

Staff entered the new school year feeling positive and vindicated that Project WINCH was beneficial to students. Staff expected this to be a year of refinement and an opportunity to relax. This was also the end of their three-year Chapter 1 schoolwide improvement grant. Test scores at year's end showed no improvement over the previous year's twelve NCE points gain. The state said Overland would not be funded for another three-year cycle because it failed to meet its achievement targets. Interestingly, the state recanted and refunded Project WINCH for another three years.

The key to the success of the project is the involvement and sense of ownership on the part of the staff. It's their program and they're going to do everything to make sure it works. **Bushman**

Bushman suggests several reasons. First, the project was receiving very positive attention throughout the state, making it politically risky to end funding. Second, the small number of students tested raised questions about test result validity. The state agreed to rethink how to accurately assess learning at the school. For the Overland staff, three more years as a Chapter 1 school-improvement project meant freedom to continue their program, additional staff-development opportunities, and some increased funding.

The 1993-94 school year: Looking toward the future

Overland Elementary will be closed at the end of 1995-96 school year. Plans are under way to transfer the staff to another elementary school located nearby (on the other side of the tracks). The principal and staff are working on a plan that would make Project WINCH a magnet program, drawing students from all over the county. The only thing that is assured is the continuation of the program in some form. Bushman says the staff will work to refine assessment in light of program emphasis on writing and problem solving. There is also an effort to increase the depth of thematic instruction to ensure greater integration of content across the five learning centers.

Ownership: The Key to Problem Solution

"The key to the success of the project," Bushman believes, "is the involvement and sense of ownership on the part of the staff. It's their program and they're going to do everything to make sure it works." Because of this strong sense of ownership and Bushman's leadership style, the staff has felt empowered to collectively address problems and challenges as they have surfaced, without having solutions imposed on them from outside the school. Teachers unanimously see Bushman as an integral element of the school's problem-solving approach. Problems faced by the staff, Bushman says, "have been frequent, but generally minor in nature." He identifies five problem areas:

1. *Personalities and decision-making structure.* The staff is small and close knit. "If you don't fit in," says Bushman, "the staff will generally exert pressure in a subtle but effective manner until a change occurs." In addition, "there exists a kind of fluid, loose, staff-centered style of decision-making that works well for some and is deadly for others."

2. *Curriculum alignment and assessment.* Program evaluation has been based, primarily, on standardized achievement. These measures do not reflect the nature of classroom instruction or content. Moreover, they are not sensitive to affective outcomes.

3. *Changing staff assignments.* The program is organized around five learning centers, with one teacher assigned to each center. Staff members changed assignments on numerous occasions to emphasize their strengths and better meet the needs of students. These changes may contribute to a lack of continuity.

4. *Curriculum integration.* Because teachers are organized as subject-area specialists with their own rooms and programs, the integration of math, reading, science, and the other content areas is problematic. Teachers collaborate on using common themes across subject areas, but curricular challenges persist. "Sometimes the curriculum seems a bit disjointed," Bushman says.

5. *Slipping back into a graded frame of reference.* External pressures to show improvement in test scores and the complexity of the multiage classroom have caused the staff to occasionally fall back into viewing students from a grade-level perspective.

The principal's there and I can go talk to him without feeling judged or that my job is in jeopardy. **McCarty**

For the most part, instructional staff concur with Bushman's analysis. However, there are noteworthy exceptions.

Problems seen through teachers' eyes

Change and the change process bring with them as much trauma as excitement, insecurity as empowerment, and doubt as exhilaration. At Overland, most teachers portrayed change as traumatic. "When we first started out, we felt like first-year teachers," Craner says. "I

mean, it was hard." McCarty, who runs the reading and writing center, says the changes also triggered self-doubt about his abilities in the classroom. "There were days that I remember going home in tears and telling my wife, 'I don't know how to teach anymore. I don't know what I'm doing anymore'." Those sentiments were echoed by the special-education teacher. "I didn't know what I was doing at first," she says. "I didn't know if I was supposed to be in the room or if I was supposed to pull kids out."

There were days that I remember going home in tears and telling my wife, "I don't know how to teach anymore. I don't know what I'm doing anymore." **McCarty**

During interviews, teachers most often mentioned the challenges posed by the broad range of developmental levels in their multiage classrooms, where an at-risk first-grader would work side-by-side with an exceptional third-grader. Teachers appeared to be caught between two opposing concepts of learning.

The first reflects the belief that at-risk students can only achieve by learning basic skills directly taught in small, incremental steps. This belief was strengthened by such external pressures as district and state standardized achievement testing and curriculum guidelines based on grade level. The assumption underlying this approach rests on the belief that students cannot process information at higher order levels of thinking without first mastering basic skills.

Although there is merit to learning basic skills, there is no evidence suggesting higher order thinking depends on mastering these skills. Moreover, textbook-driven methods of teaching basic skills tend to rob students of their desire to learn.

The second conception of learning appeared to grow from staff frustration with student failure. Project WINCH was born from this frustration and reflects a significant reorientation to learning. Staff sought to provide learning experiences generally associated with the accelerated or talented-and-gifted students. Instruction involved a major emphasis on cooperative learning, enrichment, and other interactive forms of instruction. Teachers faced major changes in their expectations and the way they delivered curriculum.

For the majority of staff members, implementing WINCH meant unlearning powerfully held notions about how children learn. For example, McCarty describes the difficulty he had resolving the tension between his focus on basic reading skills and what he calls enrichment.

> I had the responsibility of seeing that students had a certain level of skills, but I'm not sure I ever resolved this need. I knew that if I started with the enrichment activities, that the projects and different activities would provide students the skills they needed. Then I would see something really lacking and I would go to a skill page.

When asked what approach to learning worked best with his students, McCarty said, "The enrichment, the project, or activities. They definitely learn more. They liked it more, so they're more receptive."

> *You have to change your way of thinking. It's kind of a struggle, especially if you've taught for years and years and you're ingrained in that old way. I was one of those teachers—I didn't want Johnny copying off Mary. That was a no-no. And now, that's how children learn. I finally learned that after all these years.*
> **H. Craner**

Teachers said that several factors influenced the stress they felt in making the transition to multiage teaching. For example, experienced teachers conveyed a sense of feeling more frustrated than their less-experienced colleagues. Furthermore, teachers said subjects such as math and reading were more stressful than subjects such as science, social studies, and writing, where content was viewed as less skills-dependent or convergent.

Staff invariably mentioned Nilene Turner, the science teacher, as a person who had the best grasp on multiage curriculum. Teachers, Turner says, must let go of control in the classroom and provide experiential, hands-on learning opportunities for students. "We've put them in little groups, we work with them, we do a lot of hands-on things," she says. "But I'm also trying to have more things in the room that they can go and just experiment with. . . not so much that I'm controlling it."

Parent relations and community

By all accounts, parent relations have been positive and supportive. However, their actual involvement has been minimal. Two main reasons have been suggested. First, many parents have had poor experiences in school themselves and feel intimidated by educators. Second, it is difficult for parents to come into the school because of work and other obligations.

If the teachers, the principal, and the parents are really interested in what's best for the children and want them to grow and develop into decent human beings and not problems, they will try to work together. Because with today's changing times, we have to. **McElhinney**

The school has struggled with this problem by offering parent conferences at times that would not conflict with work

hours. Results have been mixed, but efforts continue. "You have to have parent involvement," says Turner. "You just keep trying." To build support and improve relationships among Overland's sizable Hispanic community, Bushman received funding for a home-school coordinator.

It's nice to have the support always there. And if you don't have it, I don't think you can survive. You just won't make it. **Bushman**

Occasionally, Overland staff has felt ostracized from the rest of the school district. On the one hand, it has received extra resources to carry out its mission as well as praise from outside the district for its multiage project. This, in turn, has created additional pressure to demonstrate program viability. Bushman has consciously cultivated allies at state and local levels to protect his staff and program from potentially damaging community influences.

"You've got to be ready for that pebble in the pond when things come back to you," he says. This means building support "everywhere along the line—the superintendent all the way up to the governor. Unfortunately, it doesn't happen naturally. You have to work on it constantly and establish those relationships all the way along the line."

Benefits Have Outweighed Difficulties

Project WINCH has been a catalyst in transforming the educational beliefs and practices of everyone involved in the project. Table 10 summarizes the rewards and benefits that have helped sustain the project for more than four years. Central to all comments is the powerful place rewards play in teacher experiences. Respondents unanimously felt teaching to be more rewarding. Students seemed more confident and motivated to learn. Friendships emerged across all age levels, and new interpersonal norms emerged in the school. Students demonstrated a willingness to give and receive help, especially in terms of older students modeling for the younger ones.

I sent a couple of fourth-graders down to help a first-grader for a few minutes a day. And when they went out for recess, that student was their friend, and they could talk to them, less fighting, less things went on in the playground, because all of a sudden it wasn't, "He's a first-grader! Ha, ha, ha!" Now "he's my friend." And there was a big change. **T. Craner**

Parents who were interviewed said their children were better off because the multiage program was instrumental in helping to develop leadership and an appreciation for cultural and developmental diversity. For example, Sandra Beabout, whose son has been with the program since its inception, believes it is "good for kids to know other cultures and to experience working with older and younger students. There are things to learn and things to teach. This is something a child can use as he develops throughout life."

In many ways, the multiage environment has made teaching easier. It has helped reduce class size. It has provided teachers with an opportunity to learn more about their students and to better understand their individual learning styles. It has eliminated retention and provided an environment where all children can succeed at their own developmental level. However, the most often-mentioned advantage, and a key element in program success, has been the use of peer learning as an instructional tool.

In past years, teachers followed the dominant instructional paradigm that placed them as the controlling center of the classroom. To maintain order and discipline, students were seldom allowed to help each other or work in small groups. Once teachers were given license to share control with students, motivation and learning began to improve. "If you walk into any of the learning centers, the desks are not in rows anymore," notes a first-grade teacher. "Teachers have become less dominant, and children have become more in-

Table 10

Perceived Benefits of Multiage Teaching for Teachers and Students (ranked from most frequently mentioned to least frequently mentioned) Overland Elementary School

Benefits for Teachers	*Benefits for Students*
Improves the rewards for teaching and eliminates criticism from other district staff over poor achievement results.	Builds self-esteem and confidence by exposing students to a wide variety of curriculum and by varying learning experiences: group work, conflict management, hands-on math and science, and so forth.
Reduces class size by distributing students across the five learning centers.	Creates a family-like atmosphere where students learn to help one another and have cross-age friendships.
Creates continuity across years so teachers can build on knowledge learned in the past.	Creates an environment where every child can succeed by eliminating retention and allowing children to develop at their own rate.
Creates an environment where every child can succeed by eliminating retention and allowing children to develop at their own rate.	Motivates students and helps build confidence by exposing them to a variety of teachers.
	Improves student behavior through peer modeling and leadership opportunities.
Improves student behavior through peer modeling and leadership opportunities.	Teaches students to accept and value diversity.
Topics Mentioned Less Than Twice	**Topics Mentioned Less Than Twice**
Reduces pullouts to a minimum, thereby eliminating tendency to fragment the child's learning and the program.	Reduces pullouts to a minimum, thereby eliminating tendency to fragment the child's learning and the program.
Increases staff cohesion and school unity.	
Learning center format allows teachers to use their time more efficiently.	
Increases the amount of one-to-one that is possible (using other students and teachers).	

volved. They have more say in what's going on." For example, Hispanic students were encouraged to use Spanish to help peers understand concepts presented in English. It may be that actively promoting peer interaction and learning has been the most powerful instructional strategy employed by the Overland staff.

We're looking more for the way to work out the answers and work out the process. I see people getting together and discussing more issues and sharing more things.
Bywater

The project has also improved instruction by creating conditions in which teacher collaboration can flourish. For example, Craner describes the situation of Jesse, a very large fourth-grade boy functioning at the second-grade level. On his first day of school, he plopped down into a chair, refusing to change seats when asked by the teacher. Craner says:

> Jesse went through the program and he plopped and he plopped until one day in the faculty lounge we said, "What are we going to do with Jesse?" We brainstormed at lunch time or whenever we were together. Before, if he was just in my room, I would be the only one concerned. But now we're all concerned because we all see him. I would tell what I found worked with Jesse. And then somebody else would say,

"Well, this is working." After a while, Jesse didn't plop any more. Jesse came in and Jesse started to be enthusiastic. Jesse started to participate.

For the majority of school staff members, project WINCH ushered in changes in their professional lives, and, like Jesse, they underwent a positive transformation in attitude and behavior toward their work lives. Norms of professional isolation, competition, and a territorial behavior toward curriculum gave way to norms of collaboration and cooperation among staff. Further, an expansive view of curriculum emerged that placed students rather than grade level at the center of instructional decisions.

Boise-Eliot School

*B*oise-Eliot School, located in the heart of Portland, Oregon's innercity, serves more than 700 students in preschool through fifth grades. In 1964, the school became an early childhood learning center and was later remodeled to optimize the use of space for young children. The school currently offers six full-day kindergartens and five half-day prekindergarten classrooms. These programs focus on the social, emotional, physical, and cognitive needs of innercity children. Boise-Eliot is also an early childhood magnet school, drawing children from all over the city. Its student population includes a rich cultural mix of African-American, Caucasian, Hispanic, Native American, and Asian children and their parents and families.

The school philosophy and mission statement place the child in the center of learning and decision-making. The needs of the child are always the determining factor underlying the solution of any problem. Moreover, learning is emphasized as a lifelong activity encompassing all aspects of the child's life. Extensive parent and family involvement opportunities are also provided. These opportunities include parenting classes, a grandparent support group, and inschool child care to support parents who volunteer in the classroom. Of significant interest is the inclusive nature of how the school defines the terms *involvement*, *family*, and *parents* to maximize the important influences in children's lives:

> *Involvement* is any way a family helps a child to learn. All involvement by family or friends is valued, whether it is to encourage regular attendance or to volunteer hundreds of hours of classroom time.
>
> *Parent and family* can be defined as the caregivers and friends who are in an extended family who interact in any way to encourage the child in the learning process. Parents, family, and friends are the child's first teachers before they enter school. The school staff are co-teachers. (Boise-Eliot 1994, p.1)

Boise-Eliot reflects these beliefs. In the entryway to this two-story remodeled brick school, a large scoreboard displays school goals and tracks the degree to which they have been achieved. Hallways are wide, spacious, and reflect constant student use. For example, learning center areas—a minikitchen, small-group work areas, and art centers—are located throughout the hallways. A dental facility provides inschool examinations for students. Bulletin boards portray a range of themes—from a celebration of the cultural diversity of the school and community to examples of student writing and science projects. Many displays emphasize self-esteem-building activities, showing pictures of students and their families. Everywhere, displays reflect the value of children in relationships with other people.

Principal Betty Campbell has been at Boise-Eliot for more than eleven years. In that time, the school and Campbell have earned a reputation for excellence in education and commitment to children and their families.* Campbell has been instrumental in establishing school norms supportive of improvement and innovation. Says Erin Cason, a teacher with twenty years of teaching in Portland's innercity:

> There's a sense of having lots of support schoolwide. One of the neat things about this school is that innovation and going your own direction have always been encouraged and always been accepted. No one would feel that they were setting themselves apart or in any way becoming outcasts by saying, "I want to do this," just because it was different from what other people might be doing. And there is enough momentum right now toward multiage and administrative support behind

the concept that it was very comfortable going in this direction. There was no level of discomfort at all.

Many changes reflect elements found in multiage programs. For example, developmentally appropriate practice (DAP) is a mainstay of the instructional program. Numerous teachers remain with their same classes over several years of instruction to enhance the stability in the lives of children with many needs.* Pullout programs have either been eliminated or modified to reduce instructional fragmentation. Teachers collaborate for the purposes of instructional planning, teaching, and decision-making.

In such a climate, one would expect the implementation of multiage organization to be rapid and unconstrained. However, district and school size, leadership style, and the complexity of working in a culturally diverse, innercity community have placed constraints on the change process. Thoughtful analysis and careful navigation are required for change efforts to be successful.

Easing Transitions: Time, Staff Development, and Deep Understanding

Robin Lindsley has taught preschool and primary-age children for twenty years. She holds a master's degree in early

---

*For the 1993-94 school year, Betty Campbell has been job sharing with a principal partner, Eileen Isham, on a half-time basis.

*Campbell prefers this term rather than the commonly used term *at-risk*. She feels "at-risk" implies an inability to learn.

childhood education and teaches college-level courses on developmentally appropriate practice and early childhood education. At Boise-Eliot, many people say she is without peer in her understanding and application of DAP. For nearly three years, Lindsley sought to bring a multiage blend to Boise-Eliot. "Finally," she says, "the principal said, 'We'll juggle some numbers and have you try it'." For the 1990-91 school year, Lindsley began piloting the first multiage classroom in the building with grades 1 and 2. It was not until two years later that five additional blends were initiated. Currently, six multiage blends have opened—about 17 percent of the classrooms in the school.

Activities that involve everybody have to be open-ended enough to accept the attempts of the youngest to the oldest, most mature child in the classroom. **Lindsley**

Implementation has been gradual and appears carefully orchestrated. Campbell felt essential building blocks had to be in place for the change effort to succeed. Her reasoning suggests a caution based on experience and an appreciation for the complexities of change:

> As I look at whole language from what Canada, New Zealand, and different people do, I see that it's a very big package, something I will be learning all my life and not some-

thing that is an either/or program. You don't have just one year staff development and it's over. You evolve in a process of how children learn, what the research says, all these different things.

Campbell believes some teachers rushed to get on the bandwagon of multiage teaching as soon as the Oregon Legislature enacted the Oregon Educational Act for the Twenty-first Century, which includes provisions for multiage organization.

In a school as large and complex as Boise-Eliot, and with a history of successful innovation in the innercity, the idea of caution takes on the unique meaning of care—care to ensure the best interests of children and their families are preserved. It suggests a strategic way of thinking that focuses on providing students with the maximum opportunity for success. For example, teachers interested in multiage grouping were offered a course by Vicki Swartz, a multiage teacher and consultant from a nearby school.

During the summer, Campbell offered Swartz a full-time curriculum position. "I didn't seek out Vicki for multiage," Campbell says. "I didn't seek out Vicki for British primary. I didn't have that knowledge. I sought Vicki out because she had the capacity and talent to deliver the kinds of staff development we needed for taking us to the next stage of adult growth and development." Swartz proved to be strategically important to the school's mission.

The first question Campbell asks teachers who show interest in going into a multiage classroom is whether they have taken a course from Swartz on multiage grouping and instruction. Campbell also raises other important questions when she talks with teachers:

1. What will your instruction look like next year?

2. How will your instruction look different?

3. How will you address the children who come with limited experiences?

4. How will you challenge children who come with a broad range of experiences?

5. How will you communicate with parents?

6. What will your learning expectations look like?

It is not for everyone. I think it's a very complex form of teaching, and the teacher has to truly be committed to this kind of philosophical base, because it's hard work to make this kind of a classroom work. **Swartz**

With Swartz in a full-time curriculum role, Campbell has ensured the availability of ongoing staff development and expertise in assisting teachers to answer these and other relevant questions regarding multiage implementation. Soon after assuming her new role, Swartz worked collaboratively with staff to develop a new student reporting system that reflected the school's developmentally appropriate philosophy. Grades were replaced with developmental scales that allowed reporting growth on a range of content and process indicators.

Indicators of Readiness

Campbell described what she considers required indicators of teacher readiness to teach in a multiage classroom. Some indicators related to her understanding of the change process. "I would not jump into multiage," she says. "I would see it as an evolutionary process of change that takes time and a focus on staff development." Other readiness indicators reflect content specific to multiage teaching, such as hands-on learning and curriculum planning to accommodate the increased age span. Taken as a whole, five general indicators were identified.

Commitment. Does the teacher really want to teach in a multiage classroom? Does he or she understand the extra time and work it takes? Campbell looks for evidence that an interested teacher is truly committed. She observes whether the teacher has taken courses offered within the school or district on multiage teaching. Since all instructional staff members are organized into teams, including specialists and support staff, Campbell also looks to see if only one teacher is committed or whether the change has the support of a team of teachers. "We are encouraging teaming throughout the building," she notes.

Robin Lindsley opened our first mixed-aged classroom. We waited three years before we opened any other classrooms, and I feel so happy and so proud that we gave the program that time to get going so we could do it right and make sure that people were prepared and make sure that support was there. **Swartz**

Experience. Does the teacher have experience at one of the multiage levels he or she will be teaching? Has the teacher taught a multiage class in the past? One of the teachers interviewed had taught for twelve years in a multiage classroom in another state. What experience does the teacher have with DAP, with hands-on science and math, and with whole language? These types of experience support the transition to a multiage classroom.

Curriculum. Does the teacher have knowledge and skill in curriculum planning, and has she or he effectively implemented other instructional strategies? "So teacher A is all excited, wants to do multiage," says Campbell, "and teacher A doesn't have themes and units or an understanding of whole language or have the new math criteria and guidelines in place. If a teacher can't do it for the age

span she has now, how can she do it with an even greater span?"

I think the important issue really is relationships—the relationships of children with children and the relationships of the child with the adult. **Campbell**

Expectations. Do teachers hold high expectations or standards for student behavior and performance? "In American education we don't have high enough expectations or standards," Campbell says. "In the name of process and content, we have not expected quality." In the context of the multiage classroom, this means teachers must place as much emphasis on outcomes as they do on the process and skills required to function in the classroom. Campbell stresses she does not mean more testing, though she believes that has a place. "It means that when students exit the door at fifth grade, they can do things like independently fill out a job application, write many different types of letters, get along with many different types of people, difficult people, all races of people—those kinds of issues."

Relationships. "I think the important issue really is relationships," Campbell says, "the relationships of children with children and the relationships of the child with the adult." Campbell looks to see if the teacher has stayed with the same group of children for more than one year and learned how beneficial such continuity is in building relationships with students and their families. Plus, teachers need to think about how they will build parent support for a multiage classroom. All six of the multiage teachers at Boise-Eliot stayed with the same class of students for more than one year.

In summary, Campbell's approach to the implementation of multiage has been to go slow, provide staff development, ensure "that things are going to be positive for children, expect enough of children, and cover areas that I think they need for world citizenship." Once assured of these goals, Campbell says she needs to "stand back and let teachers move in their own philosophy and style and accept the many variations and themes thereof."

Changing to a Multiage Classroom: Through the Eyes of Teachers

As a magnet school, Boise-Eliot taps the reservoir of talented and gifted children from throughout the city. And, as a neighborhood school, Boise-Eliot enrolls children from some of the toughest innercity areas in Portland. The mix, Campbell notes, provides "the biggest [achievement] span in every classroom of any school in Portland. Right now, we have thirty-nine different neighborhoods represented. So there's a great span."

It is noteworthy that addressing the needs of such a wide range of students has not been a significant problem for the five teachers interviewed for this project. Two additional factors may have eased the transition to multiage and teaching in classrooms with such diversity. First, most of the teachers had taught the same group of students for two consecutive school years. Second, participating teachers either had previous experience in a multiage classroom or had taken a course on multiage grouping. Nonetheless, these teachers faced challenges in several general areas.

Parent communication

Every teacher interviewed expressed concern about parent understanding of the changes in their classrooms. Three of the teachers said that parents had not been notified their children would be placed in a blend until the week before school started. "I knew that a letter explaining what was going to happen should go to parents when they received their letter about student placements," says Erin Cason, a grade 4-5 blend teacher. "That didn't happen. So we fell down on that. Fortunately we didn't have any huge blowups, but communication to parents is vital." Similarly, Lindsley says that the responsibility for notifying parents was not clear. "The first year was interesting because I thought the boss was letting parents know that I was doing a blend, but nobody let the parents know until the first day of school."

Campbell, though, says the confusion is part of the difficulty in communicating with parents and other groups—you can send them letters, but you cannot guarantee that they'll receive, read, or understand them. The principal says she wrote letters and included information in the school newsletter about the changes at Boise-Eliot. In addition, administrators and teachers held at least two information sessions indicating that parents would be allowed to decide whether they wanted their child in a multiage classroom. "Even when we thought we communicated well and gave parents choices," Campbell says, "they'd come back and not understand what was going on."

Sharon Sheeley, a third- and fifth-grade blend teacher, believes helping parents to understand how the change will benefit their children is a major challenge. "We still have three or four parents who are very nervous, convinced that it's not going to work," she says. "They think their kids are going to get out of here and not know anything." Alexis Aquino-Mackles, who teaches a primary blend, makes a similar observation. "Some parents were nervous, especially second-grade parents. They'd say, 'What's my second-grader going to get out of this except babysitting?'"

Clearly, given the importance of parental understanding and support, educators should not assume parents receive information or that they understand it. Like any learners, parents will vary in how they process information and what they understand. To be effective, communication must be ongoing and multidimensional, drawing on diverse approaches to ensure understanding.

Staff relations and support

Lindsley started a blend nearly three years before any other staff member. This created several problems. She felt isolated from other teachers. Her classroom reflected many developmentally appropriate practices that departed radically from what other teachers perceived as effective teaching. Students actively engaged in projects, buddy reading, learning centers, and so forth, which some teachers viewed as play. "It was a little bit threatening to people at first," Swartz says. "Were they to move in this direction as well? And would they still be considered good teachers in the eyes of the principal and people they care about in the building if they chose to not go mixed age?"

In many ways, Lindsley found herself like a left-handed person in a right-handed world. "Being the only one doing a blend creates problems in communication," she says. "I can't go next door and say, 'Well, what are you doing in math?' It won't help you to go next door because they're not doing math with a range like mine." Interestingly, nearly every new blend started since Lindsley piloted the first blend has been implemented by teacher teams.

Adapting curriculum

Teachers mentioned two problems in this area. The first relates to the rotation of grade-level content and themes to ensure required content is covered and to avoid repetition. Erin Cason, who characterizes herself as well organized, found curriculum planning to be her biggest challenge. "Curriculum planning was like the wall in front of the carrot," she says. "How am I going to get through that? Do I really want to put myself into doing this much extra work? Oh, my God! I've got another year's curriculum to plan. The issue was, 'I have one year of lesson plans; I need two!'" Cason and her teaching partner, Anne Hasson, collaborated in developing the outline of a two-year instructional plan. Within the first month of school, her curriculum concerns melted away. "My issues now are standard teacher-type issues like, 'How am I going to meet the behavioral needs and the academic needs of the kids I have?'"

Math also emerged as a curriculum concern. Swartz speculates the reasons relate to the way math is structured. As a body of knowledge, it tends to be sequential, necessarily building on previous skills and concepts. Her view tends to be born out by comments from Cason and Hasson, who indicate they have begun to group math students by skill level. Lindsley also describes math as problematic. However, her concerns reflect her emerging awareness of mathematical thinking. "I'm trying to move out of thinking that math is computation," she says. "I'm trying to integrate. I'm going a lot toward problem-solving because that's the end result anyway."

Materials and graded curriculum frameworks also have been a problem. In trying to teach to the child's individual needs and bring several grade levels together as a community of learners, teachers have found the graded materials create barriers. Likewise, traditional activities that sort children into grades, such as state testing and middle-school orientation programs, tend to run counter to their multiage philosophy.

Recordkeeping and reporting, space, and monitoring progres

Teachers also raised issues around the change in classroom dynamics that occurs when several grades are blended. For example, a teacher may be responsible for as many as fifty students. Even

*It didn't matter what age they were or what grade they were; what mattered was what were the talents they had that they could share with each other and help with each other. **Lindsley***

though there may now be two teachers, recordkeeping has doubled and monitoring student progress has become more complex. "How are you going to keep track of what the kids need and how they're moving and how they're progressing?" asks Sheeley. "How are you going to organize materials?" Both Lindsley and Sheeley raise concerns about classroom space, suggesting that classrooms designed for whole-class, direct-instruction formats are inappropriate. As teachers have gone to more small-group work, classrooms do not accommodate a wide variety of activities.

What Benefits Students, Benefits Teachers

Table 11 summarizes the benefits attributed to the multiage learning environment. Many of these benefits have been obtained in straight-age classrooms at Boise-Eliot. However, the multiage setting appears to produce greater results than found in the single grades. For example, teachers in single-grade classrooms who stayed with the same students for several years said they saw reduced behavior problems and more efficient use of instructional time. Teachers also found that pairing different grade classrooms (for example, third- and fourth-grade) for tutoring produced similar results, especially for children with a history of behavior problems.

Students are really getting a community feel for themselves, and it happens more rapidly than we possibly could have imagined. It's much more possible to get a sense of community with a broader range of ages and interests than in a small classroom.
Sheeley

The multiage classroom combines both multiple-year continuity and cross-age tutoring, but on a continuous basis and in a more natural setting. Sheeley, who stayed with her class for several years before becoming a multiage teacher, says, "Students are really getting a community feel for themselves, and it happens more rapidly than we possibly could have imagined. It's much more possible to get a sense of community with a broader range of ages and interests than in a small classroom." For Sheeley and everyone else interviewed, creating a "sense of community" reflects their belief that the learning must be built on a foundation of valued relationships.

Healthy, durable relationships

As table 11 indicates, teachers perceived their mulitage classrooms as producing "healthy, durable relationships." "The strongest part of multiage grouping rests on the bonds of trust between the teacher and the child and the teacher and the family," Swartz says. Campbell echoes this view. "We're seeing children develop much better, much quicker. There's a lot less time wasted on beginning of school things."

Having the same teacher(s) for several years creates strong relations and provides continuity in academic and social learning. Everyone interviewed felt that in a straight-grade class, nearly four months of instructional time was lost—two months in the fall as everyone adapts to the new learning environment and two months in the spring when everyone adjusts to separating for the summer.

Table 11

Perceived Benefits of Multiage Teaching for Teachers and Students (ranked from most frequently mentioned to least frequently mentioned) Boise-Eliot Elementary School

Benefits for Teachers

Builds healthy, durable relationships among students, between students and adults, and between teachers and families.

Continuity saves time in ways that facilitate classroom management and enhance learning.

Teaming reduces workload, enhances planning, and allows greater flexibility.

Students are more motivated to learn, thus reducing behavior problems.

Provides a more developmentally appropriate environment.

Provides leadership opportunities for students as role models, mentors, and nurturers, thus reducing classroom behavior concerns.

Topics Mentioned Fewer Than Twice

Provides challenge, motivation, and opportunity for professional growth.

Benefits for Students

Builds healthy, durable relationships among students and between students and adults.

Increases the developmental appropriateness of the learning environment, thus helping children be successful, confident learners.

Continuity facilitates learning, reduces anxiety about changing teachers, and increases opportunities for leadership.

Enhances learning through increased social interaction with a wide, diverse range of individuals.

Topics Mentioned Fewer Than Twice

Creates a safe, secure learning environment.

Blurs differences among children by minimizing many of the causes of status: grade labels, learning labels, and so forth.

Swartz compares her experiences of having children for multiple years with those of single-grade teachers undergoing separation in the spring: "While other teachers in the staff room were talking about their classes being off the wall and having spring fever and not being able to pay attention for more than three minutes, my class was spending three hours at a time doing independent research work in our library and had their writing folders right up to the last day," she says. "And they continued with those stories day-one of the next year."

However, as Campbell has clearly emphasized, teacher characteristics, such as commitment, high expectations, and appropriate training, play a significant part in whether positive outcomes occur. Simply having students for more than one year is not a sufficient condition for improved learning.

I get to know families so much better because of having the kids for a couple years. We really learn to work as a team, which is much better for the child.
Lindsley

Several other important benefits were described. Students Sheeley has for a second year "know the ropes" and do not waste time testing her or the system. Moreover, they quickly model expected classroom behaviors and routines for younger, first-time students. This mod-

eling provides leadership opportunities for older students. Overall, these second-year students help reduce teachers' stress and save valuable instructional time.

Lindsley says relationships with parents are also strengthened. "I get to know families so much better because of having the kids for a couple years," she says. "We really learn to work as a team, which is much better for the child."

Facilitating the developmentally appropriate environment

The multiage classroom facilitates developmental opportunities for children, especially when teachers capitalize on the inherent strengths of classroom diversity. Being with the same teacher for several years allows children to develop more naturally, following a pattern of learning more in keeping with the child's uniqueness. Aquino-Mackles says her first- and second-grade blend allows children "to mix and match so that an immature second-grader will do very well with first-graders." Sheeley and her teaching partner have had similar experiences. "We found children have a wider pool of interests and abilities to choose from, and we're able to better meet their needs," she says. This natural blending of the different developmental levels and needs of students is empowering to both teachers and students. In such classrooms, moreover, differences among children blend in as a normal part of the community. Status characteristics such as grade level, reading ability, and learning labels become meaningless for most children.

Enhanced motivation to learn

According to Cason and Hasson, learning and motivation have become contagious. There has been a ripple effect for both teachers and students. Hasson and her teaching partner have seen remarkably positive changes in fifth-grade student attitudes toward learning compared to their single-grade experiences. "The blend seems to add more life," Cason says. "The fifth-graders are not as cynical. They're not as blasé. The fourth-graders add the spark; the fifth-graders add the knowledge, and together they just seem to work well."

As Campbell has clearly emphasized, teacher characteristics, such as commitment, high expectations, and appropriate training, play a significant part in whether positive outcomes occur. Simply having students for more than one year is not a sufficient condition for improved learning.

Hasson notes similar changes. "Kids had already checked out when they came to me in the fifth-grade. They were ready to move to the middle school. They were too cool for anything. Adding those younger students has kept them very enthusiastic."

Having three brains working on this instead of one makes things just a whole lot more workable.
Cason

Other teachers perceived similar results in their blends. "The diverse ages spur children on to higher levels of thinking," Aquino-Mackles says. Sheeley, whose team has a blend of third- and fifth-graders, reports that "third-graders are learning faster about things and the parents are giving us feedback about how the kids have all this sophistication. There's a bigger pool of people who talk at their sophistication level. The third-graders are just moving by leaps and bounds."

Reducing the load: Teaming, planning, and supervision

Finally, those who team teach describe this arrangement as a significant part of their teaching. Although having a partner is not a necessary condition for multiage teaching, evidence from teacher interviews suggests definite advantages. Teaching partners interviewed all agreed that being on a team provided numerous advantages over teaching alone. Planning together was more productive because of the pooled knowledge and the synergy resulting from the interaction. A partner could help reduce the workload by sharing responsibilities. Teaching partners also allow for more flexibility in teaching and supervision. Sheeley has found that if she needs to work with a small group in reading, she can arrange with her partner to take a larger group. Finally, Lindsley points out that you can do multiage without a teaching partner, but it is more difficult because you are without someone close at hand to share your experience and understanding.

Concrete Elementary School

*L*ocated on the western slope of the northern Cascade mountain range, the community of Concrete, Washington, reflects many small rural communities that have been dependent on a natural resource. In the last decade, Concrete's timber-based economy has declined. Concrete, population 750, is 35 miles east of Mt. Vernon, with its population of 17,600 people. By most standards, Concrete is an isolated, small, rural community. This isolation, coupled with economic downturns, creates challenges in obtaining educational resources beyond the basic state allocation.

Concrete Elementary, the middle school, the high school, and the district office are located on a campus one mile outside of town. The elementary school was built in the 1970s. Its open design was common among many schools constructed during that time. The brightly carpeted hallways and classrooms feel spacious and open, and there is a conspicuous absence of student desks. Tables where students engage in group projects were strategically placed within various resource centers. In hallways and classrooms, student artwork and writing are attractively displayed. The year's learning themes—discovery, di-

versity, and decisions—are visible upon entering the building.

In 1993, the Concrete School District received the prestigious Golden Apple Award for excellence in education granted yearly by Channel 9, KCPS TV, a public broadcasting station. Concrete Elementary contributed significantly to the reasons why the district received the award. During the last four years, the elementary school restructured its entire instructional program with funding support from the Washington Office of the Superintendent of Public Instruction.

Concrete Elementary received approval for a four-year implementation proposal starting with the 1990-91 school year. Proposal guidelines provided a planning and development framework, but allowed flexibility for addressing local needs. In addition, these guidelines required dissemination of project results to assist other schools in their efforts to improve education. As a result, detailed, written information chronicled the school's evolution. These materials have been used to outline the project's development and serve as a framework for analyzing and presenting the interview data.

1988-90: Years of Exploration

Staff members agreed that changes were needed in the school's education program. According to the principal, Dr. Don Jeanroy, the biggest concern centered around retention. "Every spring I'd get a list of between twenty and thirty kids who teachers were recommending for retention, and we probably retained two-thirds of those after extensive study of the children," he notes.

Dissatisfaction with retention provided an initial starting point for evaluating many aspects of the instructional program. "Starting with that program," Jeanroy says, "you begin looking at other things. You begin looking at teaching strategies. You begin looking at curriculum. You begin looking at many areas."

From this initial concern, Jeanroy organized a site committee of staff, parents, and community representatives to discuss and explore the school program. Six questions guided their explorations:

1. How can each child improve his or her learning capabilities?

2. How can each child be appreciated for his or her unique individuality?

3. How can school be structured to accommodate children who learn at differing rates and are developmentally varied?

4. What tools can we use to help children when learning temporarily stops?

5. What are assessment approaches that enrich classroom instruction and enable children to demonstrate their true competencies?

6. How can the entire Concrete community, including parents, business people, and others deepen their involvement at the Concrete Elementary School?

In seeking to answer these questions, the site committee, over a two-year period, identified problem areas and potential solutions, designed multiage concepts, shared their research, and obtained support from colleagues and the community. The net result was a grant proposal under the state's Schools for the Twenty-First Century Program. The school received funding to achieve four goals and related activities.

Goal 1. To restructure Concrete Elementary into a nongraded, continuous-progress school:

• Students will be organized into multiage clusters.

• Teachers will be organized into teams, with each team responsible for a cluster.

• Student needs will determine the curriculum, the materials, and the number of children to be engaged in any given educational experience.

- Student progress will be continuous and self-paced according to student-written goals, needs, and development without regard to grade level.

- There will be no procedures for retention or promotion, but there will be procedures for continuous student progress and reporting.

- Testing and monitoring of progress will be continual and integrated as a natural expression of what has been learned.

- Release time and staff development will be provided.

These activities were scheduled for implementation over four years: 1990-91, design new program; 1991-92, first-, second-, and third-grade classrooms adopt the continual progress format; 1992-93, fourth-grade classrooms adopt the new format; 1993-94, fifth-grade classrooms adopt new format.

Goal 2: To provide teachers and parents with tools to assist children when their learning temporarily stops:

- Teachers and parent volunteers will be taught research-based cognitive learning skills and strategies for use in facilitating student learning. Methods will include observation and assessment skills, instructional processes, and tools for developing student-learning programs.

- Students will be taught independent learning skills that will help them become life-long learners.

Goal 3: To deepen the involvement of Concrete community members at the Concrete Elementary School:

- Policy development will outline and legitimize parental involvement through site-based management teams.

- Administrative financial support will be provided to help implement parent programs.

- Parents will be engaged as partners by extending the concept of a community learning center and offering workshops on a range of topics appropriate to program goals, such as parenting skills, literacy education, and skills in life-long learning.

- A mentoring program will be provided for students with local businesses.

Goal 4. To replace traditional forms of assessment with competency-based assessment:

- New student assessment and evaluation reporting procedures appropriate to the continuous-progress program will be developed.

Additionally, a staff-incentive-pay plan incorporated three key elements designed to enhance intrinsic motivation and ownership in the program. These included: (1) formation of collaborative workgroups with decision-making authority regarding details of the program, (2) extra pay for program-related hours beyond the regular work-day, and (3) extensive staff development aligned with program goals. An underlying objective, according to proposal documents, was to "stimulate greater teacher participation in school affairs and decision-making policies as well as encourage higher levels of performance" (Concrete Elementary School, 1989, p. 19).

One of the things that was the most helpful to me was to go to some other schools, see what they were trying, see what they've done, see what was working and what wasn't working, and talk to the teachers. **Hein**

This objective also embodies many of the same outcomes desired for students. The site committee intended the concept of continuous progress in learning to include the staff and the community. In this way, a community of learners could be developed that would cut across age, role, and occupation. The proposed restructuring plan received assurances of cooperation and compliance from the district school board, superintendent, school staff, and local teachers' association.

1990-91: A Year of Orientation and Planning

Staff members worked collaboratively to develop details of their implementation plan, build relationships, and im-

prove communication. "We spent a full year in active study," says Dan Brauer, a Chapter 1 teacher and member of the site committee. "We heard John Goodlad and other people, read materials, and visited schools in British Columbia, Oregon, and around our state. Sometimes we sent teams, and other times the entire staff went to visit."

Also during this time, staff held retreats where beliefs, ideas, and desires were discussed and consensus was formed about program design and staff development. Staff learned to collaborate, began deciding who they wanted to team with, what ages they wanted to teach, and how much they were willing to commit. They also experienced and learned many of the strategies they would later employ in their own classrooms in facilitating cooperation and self-direction in students. Out of the year's activities, the following tasks and events were accomplished:

- Visit other multiage programs.

- Staff development workshops were provided in collaborative decision-making, integrating the curriculum, whole-language instructional approaches, cooperative learning, and addressing student diversity through multiple-intelligence theory.

- Design program components.

- Establish basic policies.

- Identify student-placement procedures.

- Inform other professionals and parents.

There's nothing better than parents speaking. Word travels, especially when you have a small community. Parents can spread the word about what's going on to those parents who aren't involved. **Stout**

Keeping parents informed and involved early on was critically important. Open forums were held with teachers and parents to discuss the proposed program. Some teachers found these forums difficult. "We were doing these open forums when in reality we hadn't put continuous progress in practice yet," says Marilyn Lane, a primary-grade teacher. However, parents are a powerful force in a school's efforts to restructure. "There's nothing better than parents speaking," says Lynda Stout, a parent and school secretary. "Word travels, especially when you have a small community. Parents can spread the word about what's going on to those parents who aren't involved."

The year of orientation and planning was an exciting time for the majority of staff members. Many staff-development activities occurred outside regular working hours, but the desire for inclusion and compensation through the grant motivated 100 percent participation. As a result, all staff members received the same training, regardless of whether they wanted to pilot a multiage classroom. By year's end, motivation was so high that staff accelerated the grant timelines to allow more teachers to pilot multiage classrooms. "We sat down and examined our golden year [orientation and planning]," Brauer says, "and one of the fifth-grade teachers said, 'Why do we have to wait if it works for all of us? Why can't we do it now?' And we did."

1991-92:
First Year Implementation and the Unknown

In the spring of 1991, Jeanroy interviewed the staff to determine teaching assignments. The interview process allowed the principal another opportunity to assess staff readiness, interest, and commitment to continuous progress. An instructional strand of straight-grade classrooms was offered to parents and teachers who were not ready or did not want a continuous-progress classroom.

Through the interview process, Jeanroy identified staff who would pilot the first strand of continuous multiage classrooms. Some staff members felt they were not ready for the continuous-progress strand, and one straight-grade classroom was offered for each of grades 1 through 5. Kindergarten remained separate because of scheduling and a feeling the children were too young to be placed with first-graders.

Make sure that everyone has a chance to be heard and is honored for their place in the process. We all need to feel included.... The teachers that still had a single grade in their classes shouldn't be sort of set off to the side as some kind of school within a school, that we should be blended. **Hein**

Many staff members conveyed ambivalence toward having two instructional strands. On the one hand, staff believed it necessary to go slow and provide choices. On the other hand, some staff members feared two separate programs would create division. "By spring, the straight-grade teachers came right out and said, 'We feel like we're being ignored here'," says Meridith Loomis, a fourth-fifth teacher. "We had a retreat as a staff. We talked and let people say what they thought. That brought the big picture in; maybe we made even more of an effort to make sure those teachers were still supported."

Feelings of division also emerged in the community, where people started taking sides and aligning themselves with one program or the other. However, ongoing communication and community involvement diffused any major conflict.

Staff also felt pressure because there were so many new things to learn and do. Says Lora Hein, a third-fourth teacher, "We were trying to figure out how to do cooperative learning, trying to figure out how to do thematic teaching, and how to do whole language. We're trying to do all that and shuffle all these kids of different ages in, and basically throwing out almost everything we've been doing, at once."

There needs to be teachers that hang on to things they see as valuable until they're convinced that they're no longer valuable. Those people are good because they make us think about why we're doing it and if it is valuable and are we making the progress that we should. **Berg**

Some pressure was self-imposed, but some pressure resulted from emerging inconsistencies in the learning environment. For example, staff implemented an inclusion model for special-education students that moved them into the regular classroom along with special-education staff. Additionally, staff felt the graded report card was inappropriate, which led to the creation of an ungraded, narrative reporting format that required significantly more time to complete than the old format. This, in turn, led to changing to trimesters as a means of reducing the number of reporting periods. The systemic relationship among the diverse elements of the learning environment led to many such unforeseen events.

We went from enthusiasm to the pits to some self-confidence to a sense of pride over a period of time. **Jeanroy**

By year's end, staff felt both frazzled and elated. "Because the staff wanted to jump into it that quickly, I think it was really difficult on them," says Joan Berg, an instructional assistant in Chapter 1. "It was just a lot of work, but they all committed to it and they did it. They pulled it off."

Hein sums up staff feeling at year's end: "It was incredibly stressful but we made it!" A strengthened sense of solidarity emerged, and a few more teachers decided to try a continuous-progress classroom.

1992-93: Expansion and Refinement

Results from the first year of implementation looked promising. Jeanroy noted in an evaluation report that average daily attendance was up by 3.6 percent, behavioral referrals were down by 42.2 percent, and achievement data indicated students "were near or slightly above grade level in reading and math." In addition, a survey of parents revealed increased support for the continuous-progress program. "Eighty-two percent of the parents wanted their children placed in a multiaged classroom compared to 65 percent during the previous year," Jeanroy noted in a 1992 report.

Our principal allowed no faculty meetings or interruptions for the first three-and-a-half months of last school year, and then said, "Now we are ready to face some of the other issues," because he knew we were all working extremely hard. **Brauer**

Changes were also occurring within the staff, especially with those who had been slow to embrace new teaching strategies, such as cooperative learning, whole language, and learning centers. The staff voted to replace desks with tables to facilitate group work. A new reading series emphasizing whole language was adopted. Training and direct classroom assistance continued unabated, but staff members were given time to make the changes at a pace comfortable to them. According to Barbara Hawkings, a fourth-fifth teacher:

> Those who were uncomfortable with it were allowed time. They took the same class offerings, the same dollars, the same enrichment materials, and as those materials came in, their style slowly changed. They developed, they started using some of the curriculum and the cooperative learning. So some of their styles

changed. Some of them retired because it was too much.

We got hot breakfasts for the kids. The minute you fed them and clothed them and got the counselor to tell them they were valuable, lovable people, boy, you know, they were on the road to the change. **Jones**

As a result of increased parent and staff support, additional continuous-progress classes were added. Parent requests for straight-grade classes were sufficient to warrant single-grade classes at the third-, fourth-, and fifth- grade levels. In addition, kindergarten continued as self-contained.

We try to keep parents apprised and aware of what we're doing. Don has written up pamphlets to hand out. He sends letters home to parents, various things explaining the program. **Stout**

For the 1992-93 school year, the staff worked in twelve general goal areas:

- Multiage classrooms
- Multiple intelligence (in progress)
- Student portfolio assessments
- Cross-age tutoring
- Cooperative learning

- Josten Computer Lab
- Team teaching
- Immersion in Chapter 1 and L.A.P.
- Whole language / thematic units
- Narrative report cards to parents / parent conferences
- Integrated curriculum / alternative schedules
- Special education inclusion / collaborative teaching

Staff members, with input from parents, conduct a yearly review of implementation progress. Moreover, they have learned to be flexible, making continuous adjustments to their program in light of emerging needs and conditions.

When Don brings people in now, he can say, "Here's one way that we team-teach in our building." And then he brings them to the other and says, "This is our other way of team-teaching." You know, both are great models. **Loomis**

Goal areas adopted by staff reflect many instructional elements that appear as integral and necessary for multiage classrooms to become meaningful learning environments for students and teachers. Staff seemed to recognize these elements were essential to their success as multiage teachers, but in their eagerness to learn, the timeframe for implementation may have been too short. "If you're going to be doing multiage, maybe spend a year or two working on training in cooperative learning, thematic teaching, and that sort of thing to build a basic foundation," Hein says. "A multiage classroom is not a split class."

Staff members have also used goal review as an opportunity to set yearly priorities for training. "Jeanroy's been really great in encouraging us to prioritize what we thought we needed training in," Hawkings stressed. "At our staff meeting the other day, we wanted to work on portfolio assessment, thematic/integrative curriculum, and celebration."

Staff also had to face new and unexpected challenges. The superintendent began pushing his instructional agenda, which was not viewed favorably by the elementary staff. For example, school staff members were required to implement a Josten Computer Lab while simultaneously implementing a theme multiage program. In addition, a budget shortfall negatively affected elementary support staff.

These events, though quite disruptive, also unified staff. "Last year we had other factors thrown in—our budget problems and cutbacks," says Sherry Cowan, an instructional assistant and parent. "We all had to struggle, but we really kept glued together as a school. We really did a good job in that department." Interestingly, though the budget crisis led to community anger and the superintendent's resignation, the community remained solidly behind the continuous-progress program and the staff.

At the end of the school year, Jeanroy generated a list of the changes that have occurred over the five-year period from 1987 to 1992. Table 12 provides a sample overview of staff accomplishments drawn from this list.

1993-94: Refinement and Full-Speed Ahead

The school year started on positive footing. Evaluation data from the 1992-93 school year continued to show improvement in academics, social relations, and behavior. For example, Jeanroy reports that all classes except second grade showed grade-level equivalent scores above the national norms. The greatest gains were demonstrated by special education students.

One of the teachers that we send kids to came down and said, "Boy your kids know how to cooperate. They say kind things; they know how to tell their partner 'Oops! you need to change this'."
Lane

Jeanroy attributes gains for special students to the inclusion/collaboration approach implemented with the continuous-progress program. Student average

Table 12

Positive Changes in Concrete Elementary School
from 1987 to 1992

1987	*1992*
Self-contained, traditional classrooms; departmentalized intermediate grade levels with students sitting in desks all in rows	Combination of multiage and traditional straight-grade classrooms with team teaching and cooperative planning; desks replaced by tables
A stable, very conservative, and committed faculty	Faculty more dynamic, innovative, and child-centered
Most discipline problems handled through the office with set consequences administered by the principal	A schoolwide *Self Managers* and *Conflict Managers* program in which the students are held accountable for their behavior
Staff development based on the teachers' special subject-area interests	A schoolwide staff-development plan adopted with a focus on improving the instructional process
Basal reading program with standard spelling, grammar, and writing activities	Whole-language, literature-based reading and writing program
A competitive atmosphere for achieving individual grades	A cooperative atmosphere where children work together on most academic and social activities
Traditional pullout program for special education, Chapter 1, and L.A.P. programs	Collaborative teaching and inclusion of special education, with immersion in Chapter 1 and L.A.P.
Learning centers used as a reward for successful academic work	Learning centers developed to supplement and expand academic activities
Standard report cards using letter grades and social-skill indicators with minimal comments	Narrative student progress reports using the computer to record ongoing data
Three afternoons for parent/teacher conferences, with each parent having a twenty-minute time slot	Parent conferences conducted after school each week from early November to mid-December
Some cross-age tutoring	Increased cross-age and peer tutoring
Small group of intensely supportive parents	Increased parent support with PTO participation and parent and community volunteerism
Few support services and a counselor for two days a week	Full-time school counselor, district nurse, district speech and hearing therapist, and full-time district psychologist
Little school spirit or self-identity	School colors, a mascot, sweatshirt, and badge designs
Daytime use of school facilities only	Communitywide use of facilities with an active community education program

daily attendance rose to 93.3 percent, and discipline referrals declined over the previous year. Moreover, parent support rose as measured by volunteers and attendance at parent-teacher conferences.

Because of parent requests, 92 percent of all classrooms have become multiage; all classes are expected to be multiage by the 1994-95 school year.

The kids like to come to school. My own children whine, "You mean I have to stay home? I have to be there. I'm part of the team. The team needs me." **Jones**

Activity goals have been continued from the 1992-93 list, with emphasis and training in five areas: cooperative learning, integrated curriculum, whole-language/thematic units, multiple intelligence teaching strategies, and portfolio assessment. Gary Bletsch, the last straight-grade teacher, provides a fifth-grade classroom for those parents who did not want their children in a multiage setting. For the most part, these are parents whose children were enrolled in the school before the continuous progress approach began.

What remains to be done is refinement and sustaining the program over time. The grant ends this year. Teachers were asked if they felt the school would have made the changes if they had not received the grant money. Nearly everyone said yes. However, they said it would have taken much longer.

"I think it started the system initially for us, and it got us to a point quicker than what we would have if we had not had that money," Jeanroy says. As a rural school, it is more difficult to obtain staff-development, and the grant resources allowed staff-development people to come to Concrete.

Would teachers go back to how their schools operated before the grant? "I think we have proven to ourselves that it's working and we all love it," Loomis says. "I don't think anybody would ever go back to the way it was."

Commitment, Support, and the Dilemma of Change

The process of change, Jeanroy says, is like a "train pulling out of the station—you're either on board or you're not. And if you're not aboard, you're going to have to run awfully fast to catch up."

In interviewing staff and community, this train image reflects a majority viewpoint regarding the challenges and problems of implementation. Staff mentioned the difficulty of change more frequently than any other problem. "We became cognizant of the fact that we had a tremendous workload by the second or third week of school," says Jeanroy. "And it just got worse after that for a long period of time, until we finally got a handle on what we were supposed to be teaching, and within several months we were just exhausted."

In addition to the issues of change and inclusion, several related concerns surfaced among staff members. Facing a wide developmental span of students with grade-level materials and developing appropriate curriculum and assessment resources required many new skills and immense amounts of time. "They had all these wonderful ideas and just not enough time and not enough manpower to implement them," says Cowan. "I think they all felt overwhelmed. "

Staff also found it difficult to gain and sustain parents' acceptance and understanding of the changes on two levels: (1) Direct classroom support—parents did not volunteer in large numbers to help in classrooms or with other projects; and (2) Emotional support—staff often felt that some parents were skeptical of the change efforts and did not share the belief that what they were doing was in the best interest of the children.

Change and the pressure of responsibility

The Twenty-First Century grant provided a plan and the resources for reforming education at Concrete Elementary School. Staff shouldered the responsibility for implementation through a process of shared exploration and decision-making. Once staff committed to a plan of action, they proved tenacious in their desire to succeed. However, the transition from traditional single-grade classrooms, graded textbook curriculum, and teacher dominance over learning proved problematic.

How can we make school a warm, comfortable place for us to have a retreat? People brought couches from home; we moved all the furniture in the library and sort of made a big living room for the retreat. **Hein**

The year of exploration and training gave teachers entry-level skills for working with cooperative groups, recognizing student differences, and adapting curriculum to address student diversity. During this time, staff also laid a strong interpersonal foundation to serve as a support network for coping with change. However, the training did not fully prepare staff for the magnitude of the changes they encountered.

Don has a vision and he's not afraid to step out on a limb. I think he really, in a very quiet way, is always there for everybody. We see him daily; he's in and out of the classrooms. His door is always open. I think that's number one on our list of why it works. **Cowan**

Jeanroy has characterized the early period of implementation as the "curve of suffering." This was a period when staff began to abandon familiar patterns and to incorporate new ones. Such transition tends to create high levels of stress and anxiety. Passing through this transition requires a safe and secure learning environment where risk-taking is supported by ongoing technical and emotional support. Ongoing staff development provided the technical support. The emotional support grew over time as staff relationships developed. Staff retreats proved beneficial in this regard. Hein says:

> The retreat we went to and the chances to meet and talk and sort of discover what other people's priorities and ideas and goals were was real helpful. You know there was some real nervousness about heading into this, and some people had real strong fears about letting go of things they were feeling successful with. But we really pulled together and had a lot of support for each other.

In many ways, the stress created by change helped them better appreciate the role of learner. Moreover, the type of leadership provided by the principal reminded them of the support students need when learning. "Jeanroy was always pointing out the benefits," Lane says. "He was always easing into it. He's very tactful. He's a very good administrator. He knows how to bring about change. You don't shove it. You let people adopt it as their own.

Ensuring everyone shares the spotlight

During all phases of implementation, continuous-progress classrooms received special attention. Visitors observed the classrooms and discussed changes with teachers. Some teachers, too, were more adept at promoting their programs than others. "Some are very flamboyant and very exotic," notes Mardi Jones, a parent volunteer. "Others are very quiet, but what they produce is outstanding. Unfortunately, it's the quiet ones who don't often get as much attention."

> *Don has a vision and he's not afraid to step out on a limb and I think he really, in a very quiet way, is always there for everybody. We see him daily; he's in and out of the classrooms. His door is always open. I think that's number one on our list of why it works.* **Cowan**

The attention had two direct forms of impact. First, it built resentment among some teachers and divided staff members. This was especially true when Concrete still provided a single-grade strand in the school. Second, the attention created an unhealthy pressure to conform to the new program and benefit from the new resources. The pressure may have motivated others to get on board, but it also may have done so in a way that fostered resentment.

We Did It! The Benefits of Seeing It Through

"Don has asked us if we thought it's gotten easier as we've gone along," says Loomis. "And it definitely has. Our program is good and I think we know that now. It's very successful and we see definite positive results." Table 13 presents what staff perceive as successes and the rewards that justify the hard work. Interestingly, the two top-ranked benefits are the same for teachers and students. Flexibility was mentioned most often in conjunction with multiage instructional organization.

If you put a child in a context and the context doesn't change much, the relationships get fixed, and then it becomes almost a kind of myth or stereotype. **Hein**

By having very diverse groups of mixed ages together, issues of grade-level status and academic competition are easily blurred and eliminated. Students can then adjust to their unique developmental levels without the pressure associated with graded curriculums and curved grading practices. "It's much easier to work with special students in a regular classroom setting where there are other kids who are maybe a grade below or whatever," says Peggy Kerschner, the special-education teacher. "They're just kids working on a project, rather than being singled out." Students blend to-

gether with the common goal of learning.

I feel like I really do know that whole child, because I've had them for so long. They've grown with me, and I've grown with them. **Loomis**

Building relationships emerged as an important element of the continuous-progress environment.

Teacher teams, for example, proved to be one type of relationship highly valued by some teachers because it provided emotional and instructional support, especially during the early stages of implementation.

For the 1993-94 school year, three teacher teams were built into the class schedule. In figure 2, these teams are designated by "T-T," which also indicates that a door has been created to connect team-teacher classrooms. For example, Money and Hawkings, Loomis and Hedgpeth, and Elms and Lane are teaching pairs with connecting rooms. The instructional schedule has been revised to ensure common team planning time. Staff members have sought to expand teaming. However, they have been realistic in recognizing that teams cannot be imposed, but work best when a bond exists between those desiring to team.

In a manner very similar to the bonding that occurred with staff, students have been encouraged and given many op-

Table 13

Perceived Benefits of Multiage Teaching for Teachers and Students (ranked from most frequently mentioned to least frequently mentioned)—Concrete Elementary School

Benefits for Teachers	Benefits for Students
Flexibility of the learning environment allows teachers to continuously adjust learning variables such as grouping and placement without labeling children.	Flexibility of the learning environment promotes success for all students by allowing placement and learning pace to be developmentally continuous for each child.
Facilitates relationship-building and promotes a family-like climate that bonds teachers, parents, and students together into a community of learners.	Promotes security, safety, and learning by promoting peer learning and relationships among all students, regardless of age, and creates lasting bonds between students and teachers.
Having children for multiple years creates continuity in assessment and curriculum from one year to the next.	Develops student motivation to learn and love of school.
Empowers teachers to act on their own experience, thus increasing motivation and enhancing growth and learning.	Tends to eliminate status differences among students based on grade placement and achievement.
Promotes a focus on the whole child and creates an environment driven by child needs rather than curriculum, thus freeing the teacher from the lock-step routines of the textbook.	Develops a learning climate where diversity is valued and accommodated.
Children learn classroom routines and teach them to new children, thus saving valuable time and facilitating classroom management.	Provides opportunities for leadership and esteem-building through modeling and assuming a variety of learning roles.
	Students learn more because they are stretched by their close association with older, more experienced students.

portunities to create bonds across age levels and school years. By keeping students together for more than one year with the same teacher, bonds develop that have significant positive impact on learning. "Rather than starting at zero every year and trying to figure out where students are, we already have that information. You can continue working with them," says Kerschner. "I've seen a lot of growth with special-education students in not losing time at the beginning of the year."

Moreover, the continuity creates many more opportunities for all children to be role models and leaders. "Right there, within their own classroom, they get to be on the top of the heap," says Hein.

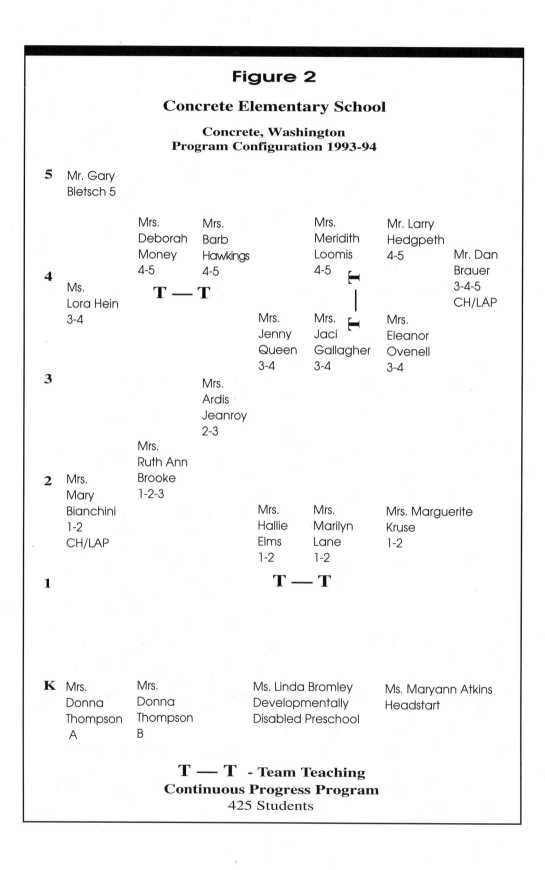

Figure 2

Concrete Elementary School

Concrete, Washington
Program Configuration 1993-94

5 Mr. Gary
Bletsch 5

4

Mrs.
Deborah
Money
4-5

Mrs.
Barb
Hawkings
4-5

Mrs.
Meridith
Loomis
4-5

Mr. Larry
Hedgpeth
4-5

Mr. Dan
Brauer
3-4-5
CH/LAP

Ms.
Lora Hein
3-4

T — T

Mrs.
Jenny
Queen
3-4

Mrs.
Jaci
Gallagher
3-4

Mrs.
Eleanor
Ovenell
3-4

3

Mrs.
Ardis
Jeanroy
2-3

Mrs.
Ruth Ann
Brooke
1-2-3

2 Mrs.
Mary
Bianchini
1-2
CH/LAP

Mrs.
Hallie
Elms
1-2

Mrs.
Marilyn
Lane
1-2

Mrs. Marguerite
Kruse
1-2

1

T — T

K Mrs.
Donna
Thompson
A

Mrs.
Donna
Thompson
B

Ms. Linda Bromley
Developmentally
Disabled Preschool

Ms. Maryann Atkins
Headstart

T — T - Team Teaching
Continuous Progress Program
425 Students

Conclusion

$\mathcal{T}$he research conducted for this multiage implementation guide was derived from two sources. A survey was completed by educators attending a national conference on multiage education and by teachers and administrators at four elementary schools in the Northwest who had implemented multiage education for at least four years. In addition, onsite interviews were conducted with principals, multiage teachers, and parents from the four schools. Results from an analysis of survey and interview data provided valuable insight into how each school implemented multiage practices.

Six questions helped guide data analysis and were used to organize the conclusion. Commonalties and differences found among the four schools were used as a basis for developing guidelines for educators contemplating restructuring their educational program around the multiage classroom. These guidelines constitute the content of the implications chapter.

Compelling Reasons for Implementation

Even though reasons for implementing a multiage program are varied and complex, consistent patterns emerged across both the survey and interview data. Survey data revealed that all respondents believed students benefited from being in multiage learning environments. Benefits accrued for various reasons, among them increased opportunities for social interaction and cooperative group learning. Furthermore, working daily with students of diverse ages, backgrounds, and abilities produced an acceptance and valuing of diversity. And working with the same children two or more years was also viewed as beneficial. Moreover, respondents consistently indicated that the multiage classroom facilitated the natural development of children.

Rich descriptions of what these many benefits look like in practice emerged from the interview data. Table 14 provides an overview of the topics most consistently mentioned across all interviews. Descriptive elements for each

Table 14

The Most Frequently Mentioned Reasons for Implementation Found Across the Four Interview Sites

Topic Area	Key Elements
Promotes family-like climate	In blends of two or more ages/grades, students are socialized into a community of learners through such techniques as heterogeneous-grouped cooperative learning, ignoring age/grade distinctions, and emphasizing the importance of helping and cooperative behaviors.
Creates social and academic continuity	Having cohort groups of children for multiple years facilitates bonding among children, teacher(s), and parents. It also increases the quality of learning time because students and teachers do not experience discontinuity and separation commonly found in the straight-grade class. Students transfer both content and class-management knowledge to a higher degree, thus providing leadership opportunities for returning students.
Promotes acceptance and a valuing of diversity	Students learn to value differences as they live and learn among a heterogeneous student population. Differences in status based on grade or academic performance are diminished or eliminated.
Facilitates a developmentally appropriate learning environment	The diverse nature of the student population creates opportunities for all students to find academic and social success. Learning is continuous. Students, regardless of age and level of performance, can generally find other students of similar developmental levels.
Leads to improved affective and academic growth	Students tend to become more intrinsically motivated and positive about learning. This improvement in attitude facilitates their academic growth.

topic have been included. These benefits did not simply emerge because children were placed in multiage classrooms. Teacher sensitivity, knowledge, and instructional quality helped to create the learning environments within these four schools. Moreover, the benefits appeared to be as great for teachers as for students. Teachers indicated they felt revitalized and renewed. In Lincoln, Concrete, and Overland schools, teachers said staff professional relationships became more personal, more intense, more meaningful, and more collaborative.

Cousins, Ross, and Maynes (1994) have identified four levels of teacher collaboration and the knowledge use corresponding to each level (figure 3). Evidence from interviews conducted at all four schools demonstrated that teacher joint actions occurred at all four levels of collaboration with the corresponding knowledge use. Cousins, Ross, and Maynes suggest that the fourth level seldom happens in most schools. Interestingly, data from all four schools suggest a high frequency of level 4, especially at Lincoln and Concrete Elementary Schools. Moreover, interview comments suggested that team teaching enhanced outcomes, such as feeling included, increased confidence, and professional stimulation. Meridith Loomis, a fourth-fifth-grade blend teacher from Concrete, sums up her colleagues' feelings regarding the transformation in teacher work relations:

> When I first came here it was just single grades. You only taught whales in second grade and you didn't share your stuff. People taught a lot with their doors closed. If teachers went to somebody else for help, it was a sign they were feeling defeated and they didn't want other people to know they needed help. Now people don't care. We have other teachers come in our rooms that maybe feel like they need to do different things in their programs. People are super willing to ask for help and to give help. We need each other a lot more than we did.

The Roles and Knowledge of Teachers Participating in Implementation

In the four schools, teacher roles in decision-making, planning, and implementing varied, depending on such factors as school size, access to staff development opportunities, and availability of resources. During initial stages of implementation, teachers and parents had choices about whether they wanted to be in a multiage classroom. Choices diminished in those schools where a majority of staff members became multiage teachers.

The degree of involvement in planning and decision-making appeared related to the personality or disposition of individual staff members. For example, at Boise-Eliot, Robin Lindsley, a first-second blend teacher, was characterized as being in the forefront with new ideas. At the other three schools, certain teachers stood out as risk-takers. These teachers often served on site-based teams and helped develop grants and pilot test ideas. However, in the final analysis, their vote did not appear to have more weight than others on the staff, though they certainly had influence. More important, what emerged instead of individual influence was the collective agreement of staff members on the direction the school would take.

Each school demonstrated similar patterns of instructional organization and delivery. Differences among schools related to the degree of sophistication and experience of teachers. For example, nearly all teachers used cooperative learning, whole language, learning centers, and other forms of active learning. However, there were interesting differences among schools. For example, teachers from Concrete and Overland

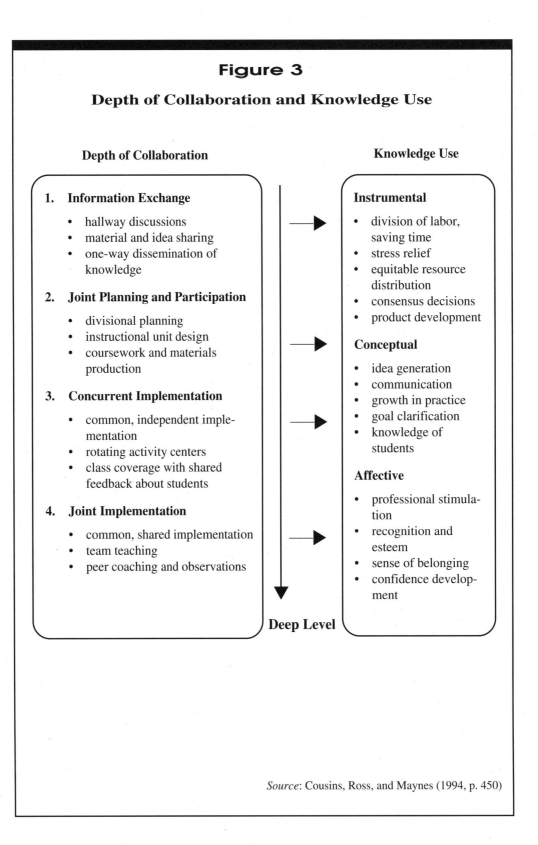

Figure 3

Depth of Collaboration and Knowledge Use

Depth of Collaboration

1. **Information Exchange**
   - hallway discussions
   - material and idea sharing
   - one-way dissemination of knowledge

2. **Joint Planning and Participation**
   - divisional planning
   - instructional unit design
   - coursework and materials production

3. **Concurrent Implementation**
   - common, independent implementation
   - rotating activity centers
   - class coverage with shared feedback about students

4. **Joint Implementation**
   - common, shared implementation
   - team teaching
   - peer coaching and observations

Deep Level

Knowledge Use

Instrumental
- division of labor, saving time
- stress relief
- equitable resource distribution
- consensus decisions
- product development

Conceptual
- idea generation
- communication
- growth in practice
- goal clarification
- knowledge of students

Affective
- professional stimulation
- recognition and esteem
- sense of belonging
- confidence development

Source: Cousins, Ross, and Maynes (1994, p. 450)

tended to learn these strategies concurrently with implementation. In part, their rural locations isolated them from staff-development opportunities about these interactive approaches. As a result, they often felt overwhelmed during implementation with the number of changes occurring at the same time. On the other hand, teachers from Lincoln and Boise-Eliot changed to multiage classrooms with extensive prior training in early childhood education, DAP, whole language, and programs such as Math-Their-Way.

Interview data suggest that the more expertise staff has in these interactive instructional areas, the smoother the transition to multiage organization. Therefore, school staffs contemplating multiage implementation might consider staff development that addresses the need for curricular and instructional strategies that facilitate successful multiage programs.

Organizational Climate That Facilitates Change

Interview data suggest that each school developed widespread norms of help-seeking and help-giving. Teachers demonstrated higher than average commitment to children and learning. Norms of improvement and risk-taking permeated the lives of teachers in these schools. These norms, in some cases, pressured individuals to conform to the dominant beliefs about learning in the school. A feeling of solidarity and trust eased concerns about sustaining the appearance of being in control and not needing help.

In many ways, teachers reestablished themselves as continuous learners among a community of other learners—colleagues, parents, students, and the school principal. Vicki Swartz, the curriculum specialist from Boise-Eliot, reflects on the importance of establishing a climate of community at all levels within the school: "There is problem-solving with staff and making a community of learners among staff, just like we're encouraging the multiage teachers to have in their own classrooms with students."

I think that Hays attempts to be open to having people disagree with him; and I think he gives a lot of power to teachers, in terms of allowing us to do what we do best. I don't always agree with him, and I tell him. And I feel perfectly comfortable telling him that. **Otto**

In each school there appeared to be widespread consistency regarding the school's mission and the purposes of learning. This consistency reflected a shared language and understanding regarding the nature of the innovation. At Lincoln and Boise-Eliot, for example, staff consistently described learning in terms of developmentally appropriate practice and student-centered curriculum decisions. Staff retreats and opportunities for personal interaction appear to have been a powerful element in the transformation of school climates from norms of isolation and independence to norms of mutual support and pervasive caring.

Parent Involvement and Support

Gaining community and parent support for the change effort consistently emerged as the number one priority across survey and interview data. However, not all staffs involved parents and community to the same degree. Involving parents requires commitment of time, often outside the regular workday. It also requires a focused effort at many levels simultaneously. There need to be efforts on a one-to-one basis at the individual parent level; there need to be classroom-level approaches; and there need to be schoolwide activities where the entire staff shares values and beliefs together with the community. All the schools studied made some effort to address all these levels.

It really needs to be a teamwork between the parents and the teachers and the administrators working together for what's really best for the child. **Tacchini**

Boise-Eliot provides free daycare for parent volunteers and to parents attending school-sponsored meetings. Two of the schools, Boise-Eliot and Lincoln, have permanently established site councils where parents play a major role in both advisory and decision-making capacities. Concrete has held community forums to present and discuss multiage issues with parents. Several of the schools include parents in the same staff-development activities offered teachers, while other schools have offered parenting classes. Concrete has a parent who publishes a newsletter describing happenings in the school and community.

The most productive approach appears to be one that is multifaceted (addressing all levels with a variety of strategies) and ongoing. Interestingly, those interviewed conveyed very positive attitudes toward the role of parents. A collective belief emerged from the interviews that schools exist to serve the needs of children and families. Therefore, school personnel must respect parents' feelings, opinions, and role as significant caregiver in the lives of children. Williams, a fourth-fifth-grade blend teacher from Lincoln, provides an excellent summary of why parents are valued:

> To be a community, working for the better of all of the children and the community and bringing in the families, is our goal. To see a cohesiveness between parents and neighbors and staff. One big thing about this is that it means having volunteers and

parents in the classroom. What I see is a community working together to educate the children.

Leadership, Support, and Transformation

Results of the interview analysis strongly suggest that leadership played a significant role in the success achieved by each school. When respondents were asked to describe factors contributing to the success of the change efforts in their schools, however, only about 25 percent explicitly mentioned the principal. On the surface, this omission might seem to suggest that principals were not instrumental in change. However, the interview data clearly present evidence to the contrary. Principals were pivotal change agents.

It's that kind of leadership. You have to: (1) get out of the way; and (2) lend a hand to whoever needs a hand, and then get them going in the right direction. **Jeanroy**

Why were principals not mentioned more often? The answer seems to be in the principals' leadership style, their emphasis on collaboration and on actions that facilitate leadership development in others—parents, teachers, students, and support staff. Interestingly, the demeanor of principals in all four schools

shared some common characteristics. As a group, the principals appeared relaxed, warm, and unaffected. They seldom, if ever, mentioned themselves as being essential or key to the changes happening in their respective schools.

Teachers have been there a long time and they know a lot of things. And if principals would just brainstorm with them and listen, why they've got a real resource there. But I think sometimes principals feel like they'll lose their control. **H. Craner**

When principals discussed multiage change, they spoke of the needs of children and families. They emphasized "we" not "I." In words that reflect the beliefs of each principal, Hays says, "I think my task is to embrace our community and have that community work together to develop the most peaceful, harmonious environment they can develop." Hays and the other principals conceptualize community as an ever-expanding circle of inclusion—the classroom community within the school community, within a neighborhood community, and so forth. Their primary strategy for building community centers on using themselves as models. They act and speak in ways that communicate the importance of openness, trust, and a belief in the individual's capacity to learn and grow. Karen Eason, a curriculum specialist from Lincoln, provides a concise summary of this notion: "You yourself are operating on the outcomes that you're expecting of students and teachers. There's no difference."

When interview data were analyzed in terms of topics associated with leadership characteristics, eleven areas were found in common across the four schools:

- Recognizes developmental differences among staff members and acts with appropriate support

- Empowers staff by providing leadership opportunities and shared decision-making

- Builds a dialogue among key stakeholders regarding the purpose of schooling and learning

- Facilitates vision development

- Highly visible in classrooms, the school, and the community

- Has a strong personal vision about children and learning

- Builds a climate characterized by trust, mutual respect, and risk-taking

- Keeps program visible

- Strives to ensure staff has needed resources, including time, materials, space, and staff development

- Possesses effective interpersonal skills

- Models personal vision and expectations

These characteristics were present in data from all four schools, but the degree of emphasis placed on them varied. For example, at Boise-Eliot, where the multiage classrooms are clearly in the minority, less emphasis was placed on their visibility than at the other three schools. Moreover, a curriculum specialist appears to have assumed a leadership role in ongoing development and support of the multiage classrooms.

In many ways, these characteristics and how they were described in the interview data suggest that principals and teacher leaders engaged in a form of leadership characterized by the term *tranformational*. Leithwood (1992) suggests leaders achieve change and improvement by maintaining a balance between top-down and bottom-up forms of power. He suggests leaders must transform schools by:

1) Helping staff members develop and maintain a collaborative, professional school culture;
2) Fostering teacher development; and
3) Helping staff solve problems together more effectively. (pp. 9-10)

The interview data gathered from the four schools clearly suggest principals assumed this transformational role. Morevoer, they empowered other staff to act in similar ways.

Implications

$\mathcal{T}$he research conducted for this multiage implementation guide provides a rich description of the experiences of teachers, principals, and parents from four elementary schools with successful multiage programs. All four schools serve a large percentage of at-risk students, thus providing many common issues across the schools.

Reasons for implementing multiage classrooms were evenly split among the four schools. Developmentally appropriate practices (DAP) reflect the initial reason for implementing multiage instruction at Lincoln and Boise-Eliot. Concrete and Overland began with a concern about student failure and retention practices. Lincoln and Concrete began their programs by offering staff and parents a choice between single or multiage classrooms. Within two years, both schools were nearly all multiage with plans to phase out remaining single-grade classrooms. Operating a school-within-a-school proved to be divisive and counterproductive.

Of the four schools, Boise-Eliot's move to multiage classrooms represents the most careful and deliberate approach to implementation. The large size of the school was a factor in the staff's decision to proceed cautiously. In three years, six multiage blends have been implemented, all with few conflicts and minimal disruption. Although some teachers may feel impatient with the pace of change, the transition from single-grade to multiage classrooms has been nearly flawless. In part, this is because many of the practices found in multiage classrooms—such as staying with children for several years, DAP, diversity, project work, whole language, and so forth—were already in place in a majority of Boise-Eliot classrooms. The school also has a demonstrated history of innovation and improvement.

Overland represents the most divergence of the four schools. Teachers chose a form of departmentalization as a means of reducing the workload. Each teacher specializes in a subject area. In general, Overland teachers possessed the most traditional educational backgrounds and teaching styles. Thus, they had to make the greatest conceptual transition when moving to multiage instruction.

Prerequisites for Success: Leadership, Commitment, Support

The changes at Overland demonstrate that even the most radical shifts in instructional practice are possible if certain conditions are in place. These conditions appear as constants across all four schools, though with some variation relating to local context, size of school, and location.

Leadership in these schools can be characterized as facilitative and transformational. Principals and curriculum specialists (in the cases of Boise-Eliot and Lincoln) developed relations and communications that were characterized by openness, trust, and mutual respect. They accepted and valued the developmental differences in staff members. They were patient and expressed the belief that all teachers could implement the desired changes. They also supported the act of teaching by finding resources, writing grants, protecting instructional time, taking over classes, being in classrooms with children, and even helping teachers prepare materials.

Their most significant role centered on their skills at transforming the work environment in ways that opened staff members to their own personal capacities for change and growth. In this sense, they helped institute norms of continuous growth and improvement, thus helping to create learning communities where people felt empowered to question, investigate, and challenge prevailing as-

sumptions about learning. Judith Warren Little (1993) has written insightfully about the conditions that support such changes:

> It requires that teachers and others with whom they work enjoy the latitude to invent local solutions—to discover and develop practices that embody central values and principles, rather than to implement, adopt, or demonstrate practices thought to be universally effective. (p. 133)

The principals and curriculum specialists interviewed all described the changes in their schools as continuously evolving journeys. In this sense, they reflected a problem-solving orientation to change as opposed to an answer-seeking approach.

Another constant across the four schools was the commitment and dedication of teachers to the needs of children. Ironically, prior to the change efforts in each of the schools, norms of isolation, autonomy, and self-interest constrained teachers' collective action. However, the development of a dialogue among staff members and between the school and the community created a collective vision uniting teacher commitment into a powerful force for change. As is discussed later, solidarity and teamwork are key facilitative factors in the change to multiage classrooms.

Finally, all schools recognized the vital place support plays in bringing about the kinds of change efforts each school faced. Staff members garnered support from a wide range of people involved with their schools. In some cases, support was cultivated all the way to the governor's office. In other cases, support came primarily from the staff itself and those parents whose children were in multiage blends. In still other cases, site councils were developed and parents brought in as partners in planning and decision-making. At each school, parents were seen as vitally important partners without whose support the change efforts would fail.

Guiding Principles from the Four Schools

Six key principles emerged from the research data. Although not exhaustive, the principles and the descriptive information presented below may help to guide planning and development efforts for those contemplating a move toward multiage practices:

1. *There are compelling benefits for students and teachers that justify implementing multiage organization:* All stakeholders spent time reviewing researched-based information before seriously beginning implementation planning. In some cases, many of the practices that proved beneficial, such as cooperative learning and developmentally appropriate practice, were in place before multiage classrooms were initiated. However, the most convincing evidence came from the kids themselves. Everyone interviewed said students were the best

ambassadors. For many students, school suddenly became a meaningful and positive place.

2. *There is no single right model or recipe for becoming a multiage classroom or school:* Each school exists in a unique context that must be carefully considered in planning. The teachers, parents, and students who live and work in the environment are in the best position to reflect on the needs of their school. Their direct involvement is essential.

3. *Neither bottom-up nor top-down implementation, by themselves, are effective:* In all four schools, change was initiated from several directions at the same time. Teacher involvement in all phases of planning and decision-making, coupled with district and administrative support, produced conditions favorable to change.

4. *Multiage programs require major conceptual change:* For most educators, especially those who have taught in traditional, direct instruction classrooms, the changes were dramatic. Even after three years of implementation, many teachers described their struggles in letting go of practices such as inflexible ability grouping and a reliance on the direct instruction of skills. For these teachers, the change to multiage was extremely challenging and required ongoing support in an environment where people are valued, trusted, and encouraged to take risks.

5. *The implementation of multiage instruction and organization is best viewed as an evolving, long-term change at the deepest levels of teacher beliefs about how humans learn:* Teachers in the four schools are learning to let go of many sacred notions of the teachers' role in learning. They are learning to share control with students. In many cases, they have faced a multitude of new experiences that raise as many questions as answers. What has emerged is a collaborative, problem-solving orientation to change.

6. *Several incremental steps can facilitate and improve the likelihood of success.* A staff in partnership with parents should spend at least one year in advance of implementation doing the following:

• Build a dialogue between staff and community about the purposes of learning.

• Assess existing practices, identifying school strengths and areas of dissatisfaction.

• Identify what information is needed prior to taking additional steps: research, school visitations, speakers, sharing experiences.

• Identify possible strategies and ideas.

• Build consensus around a direction for the school.

• Decide on next steps: staff development, piloting, exploring.

• Build long-term plans: goals, tasks/activities, timelines, who will be responsible, expected outcomes.

• Identify how everyone will be kept informed and involved.

• Identify how support will be developed and maintained: community, teachers, parents.

Magnitude of Change

All change represents a personal transition from the known to the unknown across many dimensions at the same time. However, personal changes within each individual can trigger the greatest concerns and fears. Can I do this new approach? Will students learn? What will my colleagues think of me? Changing to a multiage classroom entails far more than simply changing to a new textbook or learning a new strategy or program. Implementing multiage instruction and organization represents a major shift in classroom norms.

Table 15 presents two ends of an educational continuum. One end represents the traditional, teacher-directed, single-grade learning environment (unidimensional), and the other end represents elements commonly found in a multiage learning environment (multidimensional). Comparing classroom norms typically found in traditional straight-grade classrooms with those from multiage classrooms reveals the magnitude of change teachers face. It should be noted that many single-grade class-

Table 15

Comparison of Teacher and Student Norms in Straight and Multiage Classrooms

Classroom Norm	Unidimensional Classroom (teacher directed single grade)	Multidimensional Classroom (multiage with DAP)
Belief about student ability	Competence and ability viewed as a fixed entity. Some students possess high academic ability while others have low ability.	There are many different forms of ability or competence. Every child demonstrates competence and ability on some instructional task. Therefore, many diverse activities and tasks are used.
Teacher role	Presenter of curriculum content, grader of student accomplishment, manager of resources, and controller of student behavior.	Problem-solver, tutor, facilitator, promoting all children to achieve learning objectives and to excel across a broad range of competency areas.
Basis for determining competence	Reading ability is used as the primary gauge of competence and ability.	Competence and ability are recognized in a variety of areas. Students demonstrate competence in reading, art, music, idea generation, cooperative skills, and so forth.
Task structure	A narrow range of activities are used for learning. These are whole-group instruction; independent study; seat work; or small, stable ability groups.	Wide range of different activities for learning, where students can demonstrate a variety of competencies. These include individual, pair, small-group, and large-group activities.
Learner assessment and evaluation	Grades are arbitrarily curved and normally distributed, which ranks and labels learners. Evaluation is highly visible and comparative.	Focus is on identifying student performance strengths and needs across a wide variety of instructional areas and tasks. Growth is measured on a continuous basis and is private and individual.
Effects on learners	For low-achieving students there is a negative effect on self-concept, motivation, and work effort. High achievers are reinforced and given greater opportunities to learn. Students also develop a dependence on the teacher.	Student academic self-concept, sense of efficacy (personal control), achievement, and motivation are enhanced. Students learn that everyone has ability and can demonstrate competence in some area. Self-direction and independence develop.

(Adapted from Miller 1989, p. 130)

rooms operate as multidimensional learning environments, especially with the recent advances with whole language, cooperative learning, and other highly interactive learning approaches.

Interview data from all four schools point to changes in classroom norms along the six dimensions presented in table 15. For example, most teachers found that shifting to multiage organization forced them to address the diverse learning styles of children in their classrooms. Direct instruction, which is most effective for learning convergent content, was no longer sufficient in a multiage classroom where the age span increased the diversity of learners. As a result, teachers developed instructional approaches based on more divergent and process-based learning, such as hands-on science, problem-solving, process writing, cooperative learning, and learning centers. Little (1993) notes that current approaches to educational reform and staff development tend to view teachers as consumers of educational knowledge. She suggests that staff development is most effective when it provides teachers with opportunities to work together "in the construction and not mere consumption of subject matter teaching knowledge" (p. 135). Instead, Little says, current reform efforts:

> demand a greater facility among teachers for integrating subject content and for organizing students' opportunities to learn. They represent, on the whole, a substantial departure from teachers' prior experiences, established beliefs, and

present practice. Indeed, they hold out an image of conditions of learning for children that their teachers have themselves rarely experienced. (p. 130)

The transition from a unidimensional to a multidimensional classroom as presented in table 15 illustrates the complexity of change, suggested by Little, that each school faced as it moved on the continuum from a single to a multiage environment.

A review of the practices teachers mentioned as supportive of multiage organization and instruction help to illustrate Little's (1993) observation that current reform underestimates the amount of change expected of teachers and principals. Table 16 presents the most commonly mentioned multiage strategies. Teachers who had prior experience with many of these practices, as was the case at Boise-Eliot, made a relatively smooth transition to multiage. On the other hand, teachers who learned many of these strategies concurrently with implementing multiage organization found the transition traumatic. This was the case with many teachers at Overland and Concrete Elementary Schools.

All these strategies have research supporting their effectiveness. The fact that all four schools found them reliable practices in a multiage setting adds credence to their benefit. However, their cost and the manner in which they are often marketed to teachers raise questions about whether there may be places to begin staff development that do not rely on

Table 16

The Most Commonly Mentioned Strategies Facilitative of Multiage Instruction and Organization

Cooperative learning

Whole language

Teaching partners and teaming

Inclusion of support programs

Chapter 1 immersion

Student goal setting

Learning centers

Project learning

Hands-on math

Hands-on science

Authentic assessment
 portfolios
 performance
 anecdotal

Performance and narrative report strategies

Multiple intelligence

Student choices

Shift to trade books for reading

Process writing

Use community volunteers

Use schoolwide themes

Integration of subject matter

Cross-age tutoring

Schoolwide focus on multiage

Adapt textbooks

Emphasis on arts

external sources of expertise and funding.

The four schools involved in this study provide evidence that a good starting place may be to analyze existing strengths, resources, and needs. For example, Lincoln began with parent and staff advisory groups that later blended into a site council. These groups appeared to follow a strategy based on self-study, where teachers and/or parents reviewed ideas and research together to develop common understanding and build relationships. Little (1993) suggests such an approach helps move staff development characterized by direct teaching of instructional skills to opportunities to deepen understanding and open a debate about what's best for kids.

That concept—what's best for kids—motivated and guided the four schools involved in this study. By laying a foundation for reform based on the needs of the children in their schools, teachers also transformed their relations with one another in ways that enhanced their capacity for collective action. Rather than mere consumers of educational trends, products, and the ideas of other people, they became creators of their own work environments.

Appendices

Appendix A: Methodology

Appendix B: Data Collection Instruments

Appendix C: Codebook

Appendix A: Methodology

Data Collection

The four interview-site schools were selected on the basis of their reputations for excellence in implementing and maintaining multiage instruction and organization. They were also selected because they represented diverse locations and varied in their program design. Principals from each school were contacted by phone. The research project was discussed and their consent to participate obtained.

An initial visit was made to Lincoln Elementary School, where the principal and several teachers were interviewed. Broad questions regarding implementation were used. Interviews were transcribed. From these data a set of interview questions were written and reviewed for clarity by several people with expertise in qualitative data collection (see the section on instrumentation that follows for copies of the interview questions).

At each school, the principal (and the curriculum specialist at Boise-Eliot) served as a liaison and selected a representative sample of teachers and parents for interviews and scheduled site visits. Interviews were conducted at each school. All interviews, with the permission of the participants, were taped and later transcribed. In addition to interviews, documents such as mission statements, class schedules, school maps, report cards, and other pertinent material were collected. Informal tours of the school and visitations were also conducted.

Survey Instruments

A survey was developed and administered to multiage teachers at each school. Parents who were actively involved in the implementation efforts at each school were also surveyed. The survey consisted of demographic questions and open-ended questions about implementation (see Appendix B for copies of the survey questions). In addition, the survey was distributed at a national conference on multiage education sponsored by the Society for Developmental Education in Lexington, Kentucky (SDE 1993).

Data Analysis Procedures

The purpose of data analysis was to identify and describe the perceptions of teachers, principals, and parents regarding the implementation of multiage instruction and organization in four schools with successful multiage classrooms. All interviews, field notes, and surveys were transcribed and entered into Ethnograph (Seidel, Kjolseth, and Seymour 1988), a computer program designed to sort and manipulate qualitative data.

All interviews and surveys were treated as separate files for topical analysis and coding. Files were also organized by school, thus allowing for analysis by school and across schools. Survey data were handled in a similar manner. Ethnograph allows for the development of a codebook of topics and their definitions (see Appendix C). The codebook serves as a repository for topics emerging from the data during analysis and helps ensure consistency in applying codes across data sets.

Because of the quantitative nature of the surveys, data were analyzed with an eye toward counting the frequency with which topics were mentioned. Tables were then constructed to show those topics most frequently mentioned (for example, see table 3).

Analysis of interview data was both exploratory and ongoing, following four general strategies:

1. Data collection and analysis were intertwined. As data were collected and analyzed, new information revealed avenues for further inquiry. These were pursued where appropriate.

2. Categories were formed to serve as a means of organizing data, usually beginning with broad, descriptive categories such as "leadership." After data were sorted into these broad categories, further analysis created smaller, more concrete pieces of information using new code words. For example, Ethnograph would generate a data set for all interview segments coded "leadership." This data set would then be read, analyzed, and new codes created and attached to the pertinent interview segments. The process of analysis moved from the general to the specific, creating additional code words as new topics emerged. Table A1 contains a coded segment that illustrates this process.

As can be seen, this segment has been coded with five additional codes. Further analysis, for example, could be conducted by sorting all segments coded with "ownership."

3. Themes or patterns that describe regularities, shared beliefs, or norms of school personnel toward multiage practices were inferred from the data. Interview information was compared and contrasted as a means of cross-checking the reliability of individual perceptions of events within the

Table A1

Sample of Coded Data (SearchCode: LEADERSHIP)

#-DIALOGING #-PARENT REL #-LEADERSHIP #OWNERSHIP #-RESEARCH   #-SELF QUEST

:	then I got involved. But it was	604 -#
:	anyone was invited to join this	605 #
:	group, but it was discussions of school	606 #
:	and the principal would feed us research	607 #
:	as we could handle it, and	608 #
:	just discussions about what do you	609 #
:	think is good about education, what	610 #
:	is important, and we would you know	611 #
:	kind of springboard from there to	612 #
:	more	613 #

school. These, in turn, were compared with the emergent themes across the schools and with results from the survey data. In this way, trends were identified that may have application beyond the existing data sets.

4. Tentative conclusions drawn from one data set were compared and contrasted with other data sets. For example, teacher perceptions of the benefits of multiage practices were compared across the four schools.

Draft reports of the data analysis were sent to the principals and the curriculum specialist at Boise-Eliot for field review. Appropriate suggestions were incorporated into the final report.

Appendix B:
Data Collection Instruments

A MULTIAGE/MULTIGRADE IMPLEMENTATION SURVEY

INTRODUCTION: The purpose of this survey is to identify key issues educators feel are important for the implementation of multiage/multigrade instruction. Survey results will be used in a handbook to help guide educators toward successful planning and implementation of multiage/multigrade learning environments. The terms multiage and multigrade are used here interchangeably to mean learning environments where students are organized and taught together across ages and grades. This may mean a combined classroom (two grades/ages), more than two years, multiage/grade grouping for a single subject or an ungraded school.

INSTRUCTIONS: Please respond to each question by circling the appropriate choice in the response section or writing in a narrative answer.

1. What is your current role?
    teacher   principal/supervisor   other (specify:)

2. What is your current grade span responsibility (circle all that apply)?

preschool	primary (grades K-2/3)	intermediate (grades 3/4-5)	middle school (grades 6-8)	high school (grades 9-12)

3. What is your current stage of involvement in implementing multiage/grade organization and instruction?

thinking about it	planning for use	1st year of use	2nd year of use	3 or more years of use

4. What is your current or expected pattern of use?

single grade w/cross-grade grouping	two ages/grades combined and taught together	three or more ages/grades combined and taught together

113

5. Please write in the state which you represent: _____

6. Please explain why you are considering or currently implementing multiage/grade instruction and organization.

7. What do you consider to be important factors to the successful implementation of multiage/grade instruction?

8. What problems or difficulties have to be overcome for a) successful implementation and b) sustaining multiage/grade instruction over time?

9. What recommendations do you have for schools considering the implementation of multiage/grade instruction?

MA Implementation Interview Protocol

Name: _____ Date: _____ School: _____

1. Let's begin by having you tell a little about who you are, your role, teaching experience, background, etc. (probe for length of teaching, experience MA)

2. If you received a request to help a school implement a multiage approach to organization and instruction, what are some of the issues or areas you would want to focus on? (Probe: community support, preparing students, staff risk-taking/support)

3. What reason or rationale would you offer as a justification for trying multiage instruction?

4. How long has your school used a multiage approach to organization and instruction?

   Tell me how your concerns may have changed over that time? (Probe: Has their focus changed over time?)

5. You have been doing this for more than three years, to what would you attribute your success? (Probe: how has involvement been sustained, motivation, etc.?)

6. Could you describe any difficulties you may have encountered in implementing this approach? In other words, barriers or challenges that have had to be overcome. (probe for solutions)

7. What suggestions would you have for school principals considering the implementation of multiage instruction?

8. How would you deal with the diverse nature of most faculties in trying to implement this change? (Probe: reluctant staff, developmental differences, etc.)

9. Is there anything you may wish to discuss that I left out?

Appendix C: Codebook

*T*he following list of code words represents a sample of the codes used in analyzing the multiage interview data. A total of 173 codes were created and organized into parent groups. For example, *CLM* represents the parent group *climate*. For those interested, a complete list of the codes may be obtained from the author.

Codeword	Parent	Definition
QUOTE	*	Quotable material
SUMMARY	*	Where I have summarized what a speaker has said
ASSESSMENT	ASE	Relating to assessing, measuring and evaluating multiage programs, student progress, etc.
CARE	CLM	Demonstrating care and concern for others
CELEBRATE	CLM	Recognizing and rewarding efforts and successes
CLIMATE	CLM	Issues relating to the ethos of the school: relationships, communications, attitudes, etc.
COMMITMENT	CLM	Evidence of commitment to multiage: hard work, extra time, reputation, etc.
COMPETE	CLM	Being competitive regarding best practice
CONFLICT	CLM	Any disagreement about beliefs, values, etc. that is cause of discussion
DIVERSITY	CLM	Accepting the differences in people
EMPOWER	CLM	Sharing power with teachers, giving them the freedom to act on their own professional judgment

Bibliography

*M*any of the items in this bibliography are indexed in ERIC's monthly catalog *Resources in Education* (*RIE*). Reports in *RIE* are indicated by an "ED" number. Journal articles, indexed in ERIC's companion catalog, *Current Index to Journals in Education,* are indicated by an "EJ" number.

Most items with an ED number are available from ERIC Document Reproduction Service (EDRS), 7420 Fullerton Rd., Suite 110, Springfield, VA 22153-2852.

To order from EDRS, specify the ED number, type of reproduction desired—microfiche (MF) or paper copy (PC), and number of copies. Add postage to the cost of all orders and include check or money order payable to EDRS. For credit card orders, call 1-800-443-3742.

Each citation has a letter code indicating the topic or topics covered as follows:

W = whole language   **C** = curriculum

A = assessment   **I** = implementation and change

R = research   **D** = DAP

B = background information   **S** = instructional strategies

(1989). Special issue on whole language. *The Elementary School Journal, 90*(2). **W, A, C**

American Association of School Administrators. (1992). *The nongraded primary: Making schools fit children.* Arlington, VA: Author. ED 363 939. **B, I**

Anderson, R. H., & Pavan, B. N. (1993). *Nongradedness: Helping it to happen.* Lancaster, PA: Technomic Publishing Co. ED 355 005. **I, B, C**

Anthony, R. J., Jones, T. D., Mickelson, N. I., & Preece, A. (1991). *Evaluating literacy: A perspective for change.* Portsmouth, NH: Heinemann. **A**

Argondizza, M., Foster, D., Miller, M., Van Deusen-Henkel Cote, D. R., Lynch, A., & Reidman, B. *Big book for educators, developmentally appropriate practices: A guide for change.* Augusta, ME: Maine Department of Educational and Cultural Services. **D**

Beane, J. A. (1990). *Affect in the curriculum: Toward democracy, dignity, and diversity.* New York: Teachers College Press. **C**

Boise-Eliot School (1994). *Boise-Eliot school: Parent/family involvement.* One-page information sheet.

Branscombe, N. A., Goswami, D, & Schwartz, J. (Eds.). (1992). *Students teaching, teachers learning.* Portsmouth, NH: Boynton/Cook, Heinemann. **C, S**

Bredekamp, S. (Ed.). (1987). *Developmentally appropriate practice in early childhood programs serving children from birth through age 8* (expanded edition). Washington, DC: National Association for the Education of Young Children. **D**

Bridge, C. A., Reitsma, B. S., & Winograde, P. N. (1993). *Primary thoughts: Implementing Kentucky's primary program.* Lexington, KY: Kentucky Department of Education. **D, I**

Bridges Bird, L. (Ed.). (1989). *Becoming a whole language school: The Fair Oaks story.* Katonah, NY: Richard C. Owen Publishers, Inc. **I, W, S**

Brookes, C. (1990). *Multi-age grouping: A strategy for reducing truancy of at-risk children.* Master's Practicum Report, Nova University, Florida. ED 323 011. **I, S**

Brown, H., & Cambourne, B. (1987). *Read and retell: A strategy for the whole-language/natural learning classroom.* Portsmouth, NH: Heinemann. **W, S, C**

Burbules, N. C. (1993). *Dialogue in teaching: Theory and practice.* New York: Teachers College Press. **I**

Caine, R. N., & Caine, G. (1991). *Making connections: Teaching and the human brain.* Alexandria, VA: Association for Supervision and Curriculum Development. ED 335 141. **R, C**

Calkins, T. (May 1992). Off the track: Children thrive in ungraded primary schools. *The School Administrator, 49*(5), 8-13. EJ 441 301. **B**

Cambourne, B. (1988). *The whole story: Natural learning and the acquisition of literacy in the classroom.* Auckland, New Zealand: Ashton Scholastic. ED 359 497. **W, R**

Chaile, C., & Britain, L. (1991). *The young child as scientist: A constructivist approach to early childhood science education.* New York: Harper Collins. **C, S**

Chase, P., & Doan, J. (1994). *Full circle: Re-envisioning multiage education.* Portsmouth, NH: Heinemann. **B, I**

Cohen, E. G. (1986). *Designing groupwork: Strategies for the heterogeneous classroom.* New York: Teachers College Press. **S, R**

Concrete Elementary School (1989). *2Twenty-firsttcentury program proposal.* Concrete, WA: Author.

Costa, A. L., Bellanca, J., & Fogarty, R. (1992). *If minds matter: A foreword to the future* (volumes one and two). Palatine, IL: Skylight Publishing, Inc. **A, R, C**

Cotton, K. (1993). *Closeup #14: Nongraded primary education.* (School Improvement Research Series). Portland, OR: Northwest Regional Educational Laboratory. **R, S**

Cousins, J. B., Ross, J. A., & Maynes, F. J. (1994). The reported nature and consequences of teachers' joint work in three exemplary schools. *The Elementary School Journal, 94*(4), 441-465. **R, I**

Davis, B. I., Frankovich, M., et al. (1991). *Continuous progress with multi-age grouping and teacher teaming: A nongraded implementation guide for small school districts.* Austin, TX: Texas Education Agency. ED 337 341. **I, B**

DelForge, C., & DelForge, L. (1991). *What rural combination classroom teachers say about teaching combination classrooms.* Cullowhee, NC: Western Carolina University. ED 330 525. **R, I, B**

Dunn, S., & Larson, R. (1990). *Design technology: Children's engineering.* New York: The Falmer Press. **S, A, C**

Dweck, C. (1986). Motivational processes affecting learning. *American Psychologist. 41*(10), 1040-1048. EJ 360 271. **R, D, I**

Educational Research Service. (1989). *Cooperative learning.* Arlington, VA: Author. **B, R, C, S**

Educational Research Service. (1989). *The whole language approach to reading, writing, and language arts.* Arlington, VA: Author. **W, C, R, S**

Educational Research Service. (1990). *Enhancing student self-esteem.* Arlington, VA: Author. **R, C, S**

Educational Research Service. (1991). *Educating a culturally diverse student population: Teaching methods and the learning process.* Arlington, VA: Author. **R, C, S**

Falk, B., & Darling-Hammond, L. (1993). *The primary language record at P.S. 261: How assessment transforms teaching and learning.* New York: NCREST, Teachers College, Columbia University. ED 358 964. **A, W**

Firestone, W. A., & Pennell, J. R. (1993). Teacher commitment, working conditions, and differential incentive policies. *Review of Educational Research, 63*(4), 489-525. **R, I**

Fischer, K., & McBride, J. (1993). *Multiage handbook.* Issaquah, WA: Issaquah Valley Elementary School. **B**

Fullan, M. G. (1993). *The new meaning of educational change,* (2nd edition). New York: Teachers College Press. ED 354 588.

Gardner, H. (1983). *Frames of mind: Theory of multiple intelligences.* New York: Basic Books, Inc. **A, R, C, D**

Gaustad, J. (1992). Making the transition from graded to nongraded primary education. *Oregon School Study Council Bulletin, 35*(8), 1-42. ED 343 282. **R, I, D**

Gaustad, J. (1992). Nongraded education: Mixed-age, integrated, and developmentally appropriate education for primary children. *Oregon School Study Council Bulletin, 35*(7), 1-38. ED 343 227. **R, D**

Gayfer, M. (Ed.). (1991). The multi-grade classroom: Myth and reality. Toronto: Canadian Education Association. ED 333 532. **R**

Glazer, S. M., Brown, C. S., et al. (1993). *Portfolios and beyond: Collaborative assessment in reading and writing.* Norwood, MA: Christopher-Gordon Publishers, Inc. **A**

Gnezda, M. T., Garduque, L., & Schultz, T. (Eds.). (1991). *Improving instruction and assessment in early childhood education: Summary of a workshop series.* Washington, DC: National Academy Press. ED 337 279. **A, R**

Goodlad, J. I., & Anderson, R. H. (1987). *The non-graded elementary school Revised edition.* New York: Teachers College Press. ED 279 084. **R, I, B**

Goodman, K. S., Goodman, Y. M., & Hood, W. J. (Eds.). (1989). *The whole language evaluation book.* Portsmouth, NH: Heinemann. ED 359 500. **A, W**

Gutierrez, R., & Slavin, R. E. (1992). *Achievement effects of the nongraded elementary school: A retrospective review.* Baltimore, MD: Center for Research on Effective

Schooling for Disadvantaged Students. ED 346 996. **R**

Hertz-Lazarowitz, R. (1990). *An integrative model of the classroom: The enhancement of cooperation in learning.* Paper presented at the annual meeting of the American Educational Research Association, Boston, MA. ED 322 121. **R, S**

Hertz-Lazarowitz, R., & Miller, N. (1992). *Interaction in cooperative groups: The theoretical anatomy of group learning.* New York: Cambridge University Press. **R, S**

Hill, B. C., & Ruptic, C. A. (1994). *Practical aspects of authentic assessment: Putting the pieces together.* Norwood, MA: Christopher-Gordon Publishers, Inc. **A**

Hord, S. M., Rutherford, W. L., Huling-Austin, L., & Hall, G. E. (1987). *Taking charge of change.* Alexandria, VA: Association for Supervision and Curriculum Development. ED 282 876. **I**

Hunter, M. (1992). *How to change to a nongraded school.* Alexandria, VA: Association for Supervision and Curriculum Development. ED 348 719. **I**

ILEA/Centre for Language in Primary Education. (1988). *The primary language record: Handbook for teachers.* London, England: Author. **A, W**

Jones, A. (1993). *Celebrating growth over time: Classroom-based assessment in language arts.* (Literacy Improvement Series for Elementary Educators). Portland, OR: Literacy, Language, and Communication Program, Northwest Regional Educational Laboratory. **A, W**

Kagan, S. (1992). *Cooperative learning.* San Juan Capistrano, CA: Resources for Teachers, Inc. **S**

Katz, L. G. (1988). Engaging children's minds: The implications of research for early child-

hood education. In C. Warger (Ed.), *A Resource Guide to Public School Early Chilhood Programs.* Alexandria, VA: ASCD. pp. 32-52. **B, C, D, S**

Katz, L. G., Evangelou, D., & Hartman, J. A. (1990). *The case for mixed-age grouping in early education.* Washington, DC: National Association for the Education of Young Children. ED 326 302. **D, R**

Katz, L. G., & Chard, S. C. (1989). *Engaging children's minds: The project approach.* Norwood, NJ: Ablex. **S, D, R**

Kentucky Education Association and Appalachia Educational Laboratory. (1990). *Ungraded primary programs: Steps toward developmentally appropriate instruction.* Frankfort, KY: KEA. **I, B**

Kovalik, S. (1993). *Integrated Thematic Instruction: The model* (2nd edition). Village of Oak Creek, AZ: Books for Educators. **C, S**

Kovalik, S. J., & Olsen, K. D. (1991). *Kid's eye view of science: A teacher's handbook for implementing an integrated thematic instruction approach to teaching science, K-6.* Village of Oak Creek, AZ: Center for the Future of Public Education. **C, S**

Lazear, D. (1991). *Seven ways of knowing: Teaching for multiple intelligences* (2nd edition). Palatine, IL: Skylight Publishing. **C, S**

Leithwood, K. A. (1992). The move toward transformational leadership. *Educational Leadership, 49*(5), 8-12. EJ 439 275. **R, I**

Liontos, L. B. (1993). Shared decision-making. *Oregon School Study Council Bulletin, 37*(2), 1-42. **R, I**

Little, J. W. (1993). Teachers' professional development in a climate of educational reform. *Educational Evaluation and Policy Analysis, 15*(2), 129-151. EJ 466 295. **R, I**

Lodish, R. (1992). The pros and cons of mixed-age grouping. *Principal, 71*(5), 20-22. EJ 444 286. **R, B**

Lowery, L. F. (1993). *Thinking and learning: Matching developmental stages with curriculum and instruction.* (p. 7). Pacific Grove, CA: Critical Thinking Press & Software. **R, D, S**

Maeda, B. (1994). *The multi-age classroom.* Cypress, CA: Creative Teaching Press. **I, B, R**

Manitoba Department of Education. (1988). *Language arts handbook for primary teachers in multi-graded classrooms.* Winnipeg, Manitoba. ED 300 814. **C, S**

Miles, M. B., & Huberman, A. M. (1980). *The realities of school improvement programs: Analysis of qualitative data.* Proposal to National Institute of Education (funded as NIE Grant G-81-0018). **R, I**

Miller, B. A. (1989). *The Multigrade classroom: A resource handbook for small, rural schools.* Portland, OR: Northwest Regional Educational Laboratory. ED 320 719. **A, R, B, C, S**

Miller, B. A. (1990). *A Training guide for the multigrade classroom: A resource handbook for small, rural schools.* Portland, OR: Northwest Regional Educational Laboratory. ED 332 844. **I, R, S**

Nicholls, J. G. (1989). *The competitive ethos and democratic education.* Cambridge, MA: Harvard University Press. **R, C, S**

Nye, B. (1993). Some questions and answers about multiage grouping. *ERS Spectrum, 11*(3), 38-45. EJ 466 852. **R, B**

Olson, C. B. (Ed.). (1987). *Practical ideas for teaching writing as a process.* Sacramento,

CA: California State Department of Education. ED 294 193. **W, C**

Pace, G. (1993). *Making decisions about grouping in language arts.* (Literacy Improvement Series for Elementary Educators). Portland, OR: Literacy, Language, and Communication Program, Northwest Regional Educational Laboratory. ED 354 486. **S, W**

Pappas, C. C., Kiefer, B. Z., & Levstik, L. S. (1990). *An integrated language perspective in the elementary school: Theory into action.* White Plains, NY: Longman. ED 315 775. **W, C, S**

Peterson, R. (1992). *Life in a crowded place: Making a learning community.* Portsmouth, NH: Heinemann. **I**

Province of British Columbia Ministry of Education. (1990a). *Primary program foundation document.* Victoria, British Columbia: Author. **B, I, C**

Province of British Columbia Ministry of Education. (1990b). *Primary program resource document.* Victoria, British Columbia: Author. **B, I, C**

Province of British Columbia Ministry of Education. (1990c). *Our primary program: Taking the Pulse.* Victoria, British Columbia: Author. **R, B, C, I**

Rathbone, C., Bingham, A., Dorta, P., McClaskey, M., & O'Keefe, J. (1993). *Multiage portraits: Teaching and learning in mixed-age classrooms.* Peterborough, NH: Crystal Springs Books. **R, C, S, A**

Rhodes, L. K., & Shanklin, N. L. (1993). *Windows into literacy: Assessing learners, K-8.* Portsmouth, NH: Heinemann. ED 358 428. **A, W**

Roelofs, E., Veenman, S., & Lem, P. (1989). *Training teachers in complex classroom organizations (mixed-age classes) to im-*

prove instruction and classroom management behaviour: Effects of a staff development programme. The Hague, Netherlands: Institute for Educational Research in the Netherlands. ED 338 580. **R**

Rosenholtz, S. (1989). *Teachers' workplace: The social organization of schools.* White Plains, NY: Longman. **R, I**

Seidel, J.; Kjolseth, R.; & Seymour, E. (1988). *The ethnograph.* Corvallis, OR: Qualis Research Associates.

Severeide, R. C. (1992). *Promoting developmentally appropriate practice through teacher self-study.* (Literacy Improvement Series for Elementary Educators). Portland, OR: Literacy, Language, and Communication Program, Northwest Regional Educational Laboratory. ED 354 485. **D, I**

Sharan, Y., & Sharan, S. (1992). *Expanding cooperative learning through group investigation.* New York: Teachers College Press. **C, S**

Short, K. G., & Burke, C. (1991). *Creating curriculum: Teachers and students as a community of learners.* Portsmouth, NH: Heinemann. **W, C, S, R**

Shulman, J. H., & Mesa-Bains, A. (Eds.). (1993). *Diversity in the classroom: A casebook for teachers and teacher educators.* Hillsdale, NJ: Lawrence Erlbaum Associates, Publishers. ED 361 333. **B, R, S**

Society for Developmental Education. (1993). *Multiage classrooms: The ungrading of America's schools.* Peterborough, NH: Author. **R, C, B, I, S, W**

Stevens, A. (1993). *Learning for life through universal themes.* (Literacy Improvement Series for Elementary Educators). Portland, OR: Literacy, Language, and Communica-

tion Program, Northwest Regional Educational Laboratory. **C, W, S, I**

Tierney, R. J., Carter, M. A., & Desai, L. E. (1991). *Portfolio assessment in the reading-writing classroom.* Norwood, MA: Christopher-Gordon Publishers, Inc. ED 331 055. **A, W**

Virginia Education Association and Appalachia Educational Laboratory. (1990). *Teaching combined grade classes: Real problems and promising practices.* Charleston, WV: Author. ED 339 557. **S, R**

Vygotsky, L. S. (1978). *Mind in society: The development of higher psychological processes.* Edited by M. Cole, V. John-Steiner, S. Scribner, & E. Souberman. Cambridge, MA: Harvard University Press. **R, D**

Yatvin, J. (1992). *Beginning a school literacy improvement project: Some words of advice.* (Literacy Improvement Series for Elementary Educators). Portland, OR: Literacy, Language, and Communication Program, Northwest Regional Educational Laboratory. ED 354 484. **W, R, I**

Audio/Video

Katz, L. (1993). *Multiage groupings: A key to elementary reform.* Alexandria, VA: Association for Supervision and Curriculum Development. (Audiocassette) **D, I**

Province of British Columbia Ministry of Education. *A time of wonder: Children in the primary years.* Victoria, British Columbia. (Video) **D, B**

Thompson, E. (1994). *How to teach in a multiage classroom.* Columbus, OH: Teachers' Publishing Group. (Video) **I, B, S**

Thompson, E. (1994). *The nuts and bolts of multiage classrooms.* Columbus, OH: Teachers' Publishing Group. (Video) **I, B, S**

FLANNEL BOARD FUN

A Collection of Stories, Songs, and Poems

by
DIANE BRIGGS

The Scarecrow Press, Inc.
Metuchen, N.J., & London
1992

British Library Cataloguing-in-Publication data available

Library of Congress Cataloging-in-Publication Data

Briggs, Diane.
    Flannel board fun : a collection of stories, songs, and
  poems / by Diane Briggs.
      p.   cm.
    Includes bibliographical references (p.).
    ISBN 0-8108-2616-X (alk. paper)
    1. Flannelgraphs. 2. Storytelling. 3. Children's literature.
  I. Title.
  LB1043.62.B75 1992
  372.64'2'044--dc20   92-33672

To Thomas, who loves flannel board stories and especially likes gluing on the googly eyes

To my husband, Scott, who has given me great advice and help

And to Peg, Polly, and Angie for their valued input and kind assistance

TABLE OF CONTENTS

INTRODUCTION

A worldwide tradition of storytelling has existed in which story figures, silhouettes, or objects have been used to help tell a story. In ancient China storytellers used silhouettes to cast shadows. In Zaire and Angola "it was common for itinerant storytellers to use a vine or string to which they had attached an object matching each tale they told."[1] Today, a modern invention, the flannel board, is used in many classrooms and libraries. A flannel board consists of a cloth-covered rectangle of wood or cardboard upon which story figures are placed to illustrate a story as it is told.

If you have never done storytelling with a flannel board and decide to try it, you will be thrilled when you see the reaction of the children. Flannel board storytelling is a warm, intimate, and wonderful way to share a story, poem, or song. Because the stories are told without a book the teller is able to achieve closer contact with the listeners. Flannel board storytelling also provides opportunities for participatory and language development activities. Children may want to make their own story figures and present their own stories or retell one told by you.

This book contains twenty-eight stories, poems, and songs. Suggestions for age appropriateness are given. Also included are directions for storytelling, a list of materials needed, and color suggestions.

HOW TO MAKE A FLANNEL BOARD

Flannel boards along with easels or tripods may be purchased through school and library supply companies. It may be a good idea to purchase an easel or tripod if you have available funds. However, the flannel board itself can be made easily and inexpensively and you can choose the exact size and color.

A flannel board can be made from a rectangle of wood or cardboard. The size may vary according to your needs. The patterns in this book will work well on a board 34" wide by 24" high, or dimensions close to that.

The fabric that you choose to cover the board does not have to be flannel. Felt is frequently used and other fabrics that have a fleece or fuzzy nap will work also. The standard colors used for flannel boards are blue, brown, or black. In my opinion, brown and

---

[1] Anne Pellowski. *The Story Vine* (New York: Macmillan), 1984.

black are poor choices because these colors are used frequently to make story figures. Light blue is a color that works well and provides a good contrast. Feel free to change the color of your flannel board from time to time.

The square of cloth should be cut so that it is 3" wider and longer than the board. To avoid bunching, clip to corners. Apply strong glue to the back of the board where the cloth folds over. The cloth can be secured with strong tape until the glue dries. When using wood, staples or tacks may be used. There is no need to glue the cloth to the front of the board. In fact, this may interfere with the desired static cling.

When setting up the flannel board it should not be exactly perpendicular to the floor. A slight angle is preferred. The story figures will then be less likely to fall off. You may also want to attach a small cardboard box to the back of the board. This provides a good place to put the story figures instead of holding them in your hand where the children can see them. If your flannel board ever becomes damaged or soiled just re-cover it with new cloth.

HOW TO MAKE FLANNEL BOARD FIGURES

Supplies you will need:

-felt squares in various colors
-sharp scissors
-fabric glue
-black felt-tip pen

Additional supplies -- optional:

-googly eyes
-beads
-yarn for hair
-sequins
-fabric paint
-interfacing

The best way to make story figures, in my opinion, is with felt. Craft and fabric stores stock a variety of vibrant colors already cut into squares. Interfacing may also be used for smaller pieces and it's easy to cut, color, and draw on. Another option is to use poster board and glue felt on the back. But the pieces are more likely to fall off the board and aren't as attractive as felt.

To make features such as eyes you can use googly eyes, beads, fabric paint, or paper cut-outs. (To make paper cut-outs of eyes draw the eyes on paper adding whatever color you like and then cut them out and glue them to the felt.)

When making people, cut out the silhouette and then glue the clothes, face, and hair to the silhouette.

A black felt-tip pen may be used to define areas such as an arm or leg. But use it lightly especially on lighter colors. Try it on a scrap of felt first to get the desired effect.

Sequins and beads of different colors look beautiful on flannel board figures. If you are making a king or a queen, add beads and sequins to their crowns and clothes. Be as creative as you like and have fun!

SUGGESTIONS FOR ADDITIONAL ACTIVITIES

Flannel boards and story figures may be used in a variety of ways. Here are a few suggestions.

*   You can turn the story figures you've made into stick puppets. Simply tape a little poster board to the back of your felt figures to make them stiff and add a dowel or tongue depressor. You may also want to use the patterns to make poster board cut-outs.

*   Stories or poems from books can be adapted for the flannel board. Cumulative or repetitive stories make good choices.

*   Have the children make their own flannel board stories and present them.

*   Use the patterns to make black poster board cut-outs and put on a shadow puppet play.

*   Flannel boards can be helpful teaching tools. They can be used, for example, to help make math lessons fun or show the metamorphosis of a frog.

*   Children can present oral reports using the flannel board.

*   If you are telling stories to visually impaired or blind children use the patterns to create tactile figures. Furry or wooly materials, feathers, craft hair, beads, sequins, and cotton are some examples of materials you may want to use.

The possibilities are endless!

FIVE ENORMOUS DINOSAURS

(Author Unknown)

Five E-nor-mous dinosaurs
Shouting out a roar
One ran away
Then there were four

Four E-nor-mous dinosaurs
As happy as could be
'Til the wind blew by
Then there were three

Three E-nor-mous dinosaurs
Were taken to the zoo
'Til one got away
Then there were two

Two E-nor-mous dinosaurs
Were having such fun
'Til a volcano blew up
Then there was one

One E-nor-mous dinosaur
He must have weighed a ton
'Til the lakes dried up
Then there were none!

Directions

Remove the dinosaurs from the flannel board one by one as you recite the rhyme. When the volcano blows up put the fire/lava piece at the top of it.

Some children will know the name of every dinosaur on the flannel board and will want to tell you about it.

Color Suggestions

Pterosaur - pink body, tan wings
Brontosaurus - bright green
Stegosaurus - red and blue
Tyrannosaurus - dark green
Triceratops - yellow
Volcano - dark brown
Lava - yellow and orange

Materials

felt squares:
1 bright green
1 dark green
1 red
1 dark brown
A small amount of:
tan, pink, blue

1

Five Enormous Dinosaurs

Five Enormous Dinosaurs

4

Five Enormous Dinosaurs

5

Five Enormous Dinosaurs

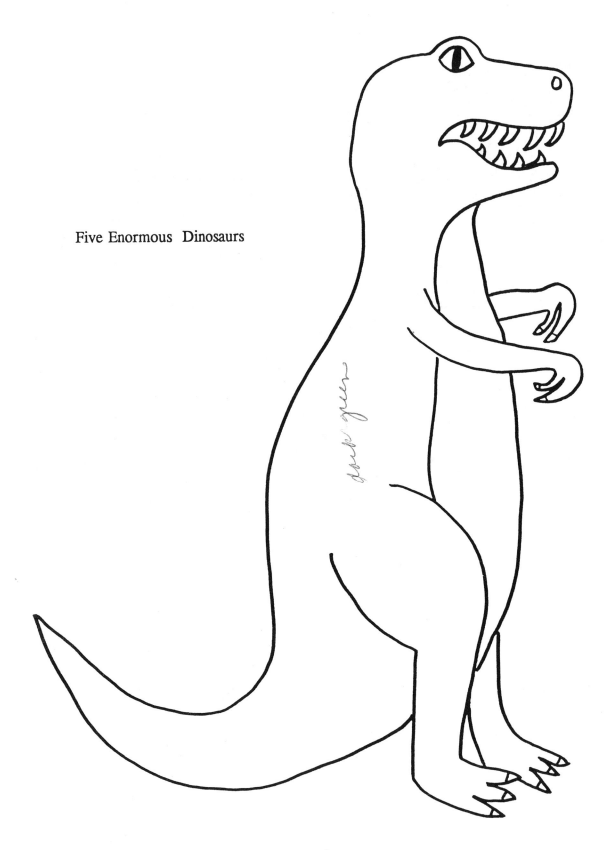

Five Enormous Dinosaurs

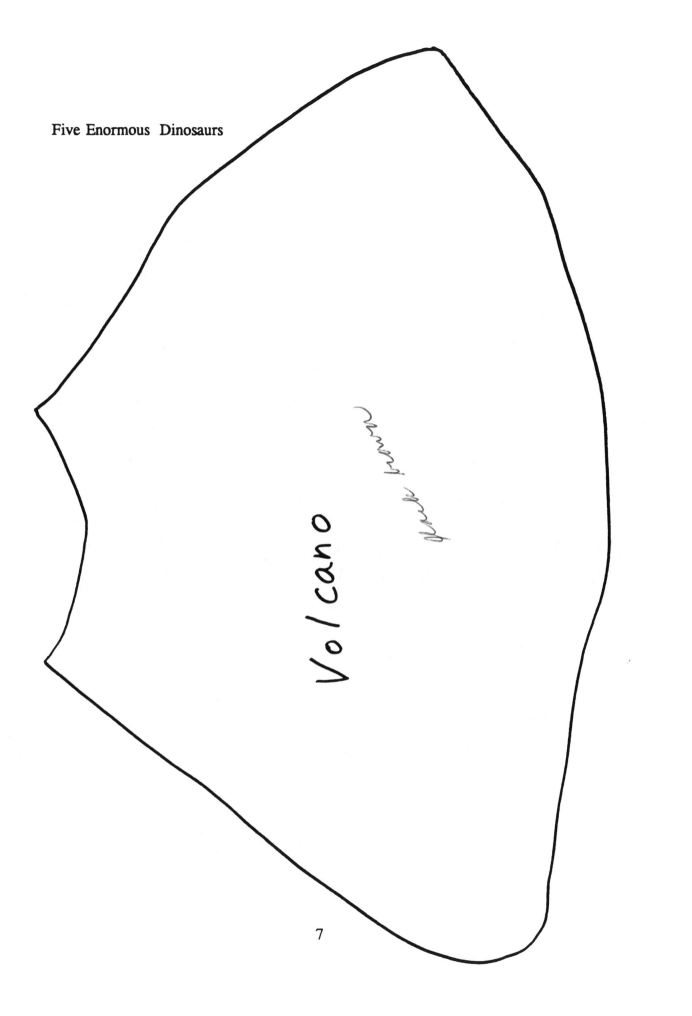

Volcano

erupting

Five Enormous Dinosaurs

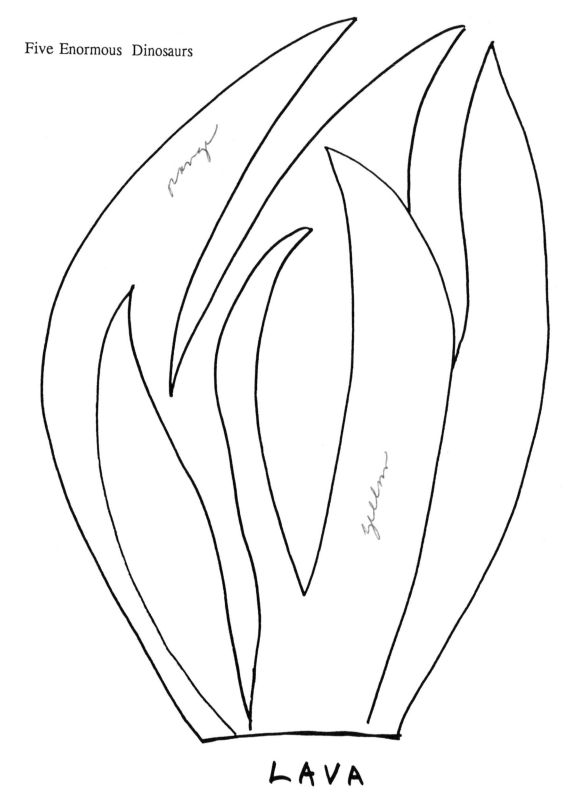

LAVA

THE LITTLE WHITE DUCK

Words: Walt Whippo
Music: Bernard Zaritsky

Toddler -2nd Grade

1. There's a little white duck sitting in the water,
    A little white duck doing what he ought-er;
    He took a bite of a lily pad, flapped his wings and
    He said, "I'm glad I'm a little white duck sitting
    In the water. Quack, quack, quack."

2. There's a little green frog swimming in the water,
    A little green frog doing what he ought-er.
    He jumped right off of the lily pad that the little
    Duck bit and he said, "I'm glad I'm a little green frog
    Swimming in the water. Ribet, ribet, ribet."

3. There's a little black bug floating on the water,
    A little black bug doing what he ought-er,
    He tickled the frog on the lily pad
    That the little duck bit and he said, "I'm glad
    I'm a little black bug floating on the water. Chirp, chirp, chirp."

4. There's a little red snake lying in the water,
    A little red snake doing what he ought-er,
    He frightened the duck and the frog so bad
    He ate the little bug and he said, "I'm glad
    I'm a little red snake lying in the water. Sss, sss, sss."

5. Now there's nobody left sitting in the water,
    Nobody left doing what he ought-er,
    There's nothing left but the lily pad,
    The duck and the frog ran away. It's sad
    That there's nobody left sitting in the water. Boo, whoo, whoo.

Directions

Place the lily pad on the flannel board before beginning the song.

Verse 1:   Place the duck on the flannel board. On "he took a bite" have him nip at the lily pad. For flapping wings, cross thumbs and wiggle hands.

Verse 2:   Place frog on lily pad. At the appropriate time have him jump off the lily pad.

Verse 3:   Tickle the frog with the bug.

Verse 4:   Place the snake near the bug. On "ate the little bug" remove the bug.

Verse 5:   Remove all pieces except the lily pad.

Materials

Felt squares:
1 white
1 green
A small amount of:
black, red, and orange (for duck's bill)

The Little White Duck

12

The Little White Duck

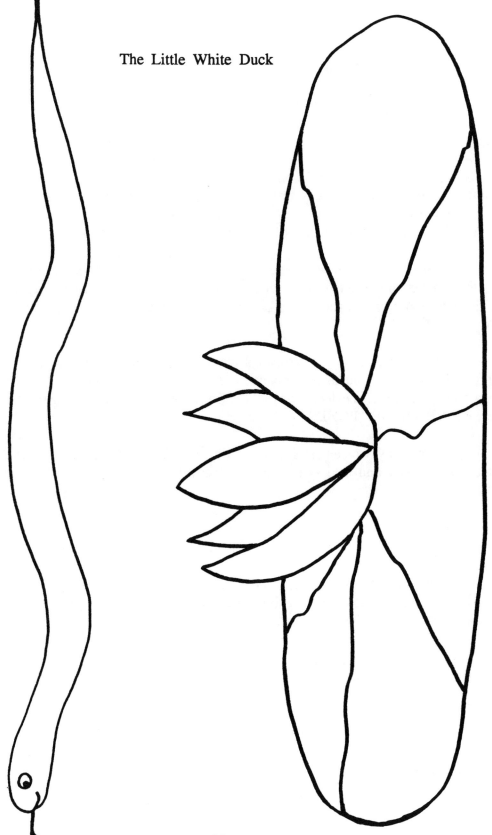

(An English Tale)

Once upon a time there was a teeny tiny woman who lived in a teeny tiny house. One day this teeny tiny woman went out of her teeny tiny house to take a teeny tiny walk. When this teeny tiny woman had gone a teeny tiny way she came to a teeny tiny graveyard. She saw a teeny tiny bone on a teeny tiny grave, and the teeny tiny woman said to her teeny tiny self, "This teeny tiny bone will make me some good soup for my teeny tiny supper." So the teeny tiny woman took the teeny tiny bone and went home to her teeny tiny house.

Now, when the teeny tiny woman got home to her teeny tiny house, she was a teeny tiny bit tired. So she put the teeny tiny bone in the teeny tiny cupboard and got in her teeny tiny bed. When the teeny tiny woman had been asleep a teeny tiny time, she was awakened by a teeny tiny voice from the cupboard that said, "Give me my bone!"

The teeny tiny woman was a teeny tiny bit frightened. So she hid her teeny tiny head under the blanket and went to sleep again. When she had been asleep again a teeny tiny time, the teeny tiny voice again cried out from the cupboard a teeny tiny bit louder, "Give Me My Bone!"

This made the teeny tiny woman a teeny tiny bit more frightened. So she hid her teeny tiny head farther under the blanket. And when the teeny tiny woman was asleep again a teeny tiny time, the teeny tiny voice from the cupboard said again a teeny tiny bit louder, "GIVE ME MY BONE!"

The teeny tiny woman was a teeny tiny bit more frightened, but she pushed the blanket off her head and said in her loudest teeny tiny voice, "TAKE IT!"

Directions

Make the cupboard with two layers of felt. Cut the cupboard so that the doors open. Place the ghost inside the cupboard before beginning the story and at the appropriate time in the story place the bone in the cupboard.

Before beginning the story place the gravestones and bone on one side of the flannel board. Place the teeny tiny woman on the other side and move her near the gravestones at the appropriate time.

Have the ghost "fly" off the flannel board with the bone at the end of the story.

Your audience will enjoy repeating the refrain: "Give me my bone!"

Color Suggestions

Dress - red
Graves - grey
Cupboard - green
Bed - brown
Blanket - pink

Materials

felt squares:
1 red
1 brown
1 pink
1 green
A small amount of:
skin color, grey, white

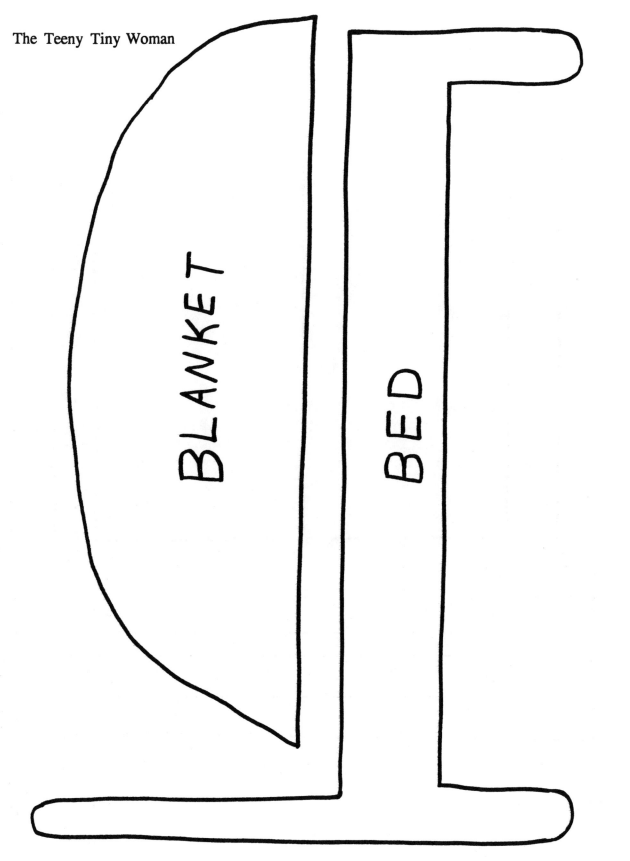

BLANKET

BED

THE MONKEY AND THE TIGER   Preschool-2nd Grade
(A Chinese Tale)

One day a monkey was playing in the jungle when suddenly a big tiger appeared behind him. The little monkey was terrified, but he tried not to show it. He knew that the tiger would probably eat him so he thought of a plan.

"I know that you would like to eat me, but I'm sorry to say you may not," said the monkey.

"And why not?" asked the tiger.

"Because I have power in this jungle. I am very important. In fact, I am the ruler of this jungle," said the monkey.

"I don't know if I believe you," said the tiger. "How do I know you are telling the truth?"

"I can show you," said the monkey. "Just follow me and you will see how important I am. All the animals are afraid of me because I have such power. Watch and see. They'll all run away."

So off went the monkey through the jungle with the tiger walking close behind.

After a short while they came upon a deer who was eating some leaves. When the deer saw the monkey she paid no attention. But when she saw the tiger she dashed off at top speed. "See, I told you so," said the monkey.

The next animal to appear was a porcupine. He paid no attention to the monkey. But when he saw the tiger he ran away and hid behind some bushes. "Did you see that?" said the monkey. "That porcupine was terrified."

The monkey and the tiger walked on through the jungle and suddenly they came upon a huge boa constrictor. When the snake saw the little monkey it started to get ready to wrap itself around him. But then the snake saw the tiger. It had second thoughts and slithered off quickly. "You see?" said the monkey. "That snake knows I'm the ruler of this jungle."

Presently a bear came lumbering through the jungle. The bear didn't appear to be afraid of anything and he didn't even notice the monkey at all. But when he saw the tiger he ran off through the jungle and didn't look back.

"Do you believe me now?" asked the monkey.

"I had no idea you were so powerful and important, monkey. Please forgive me. You

19

don't have to worry. I'll not bother you again," said the tiger. Then the tiger slid back into the jungle.

The monkey felt quite proud of himself for thinking up such a fine trick. So he, very happily, went back to playing in the jungle.

Directions

Place the tiger behind the monkey. They will not be moved from this position during the story. Place each animal on the flannel board at the appropriate time and remove them when they run away.

Color Suggestions	Materials
Monkey - brown	felt squares:
Tiger - orange with	1 brown
black stripes	1 orange
Porcupine - brown and black	1 tan
Deer - tan	1 dark brown
Bear - dark brown	A small amount of:
Snake - green	green, black

The Monkey And The Tiger

21

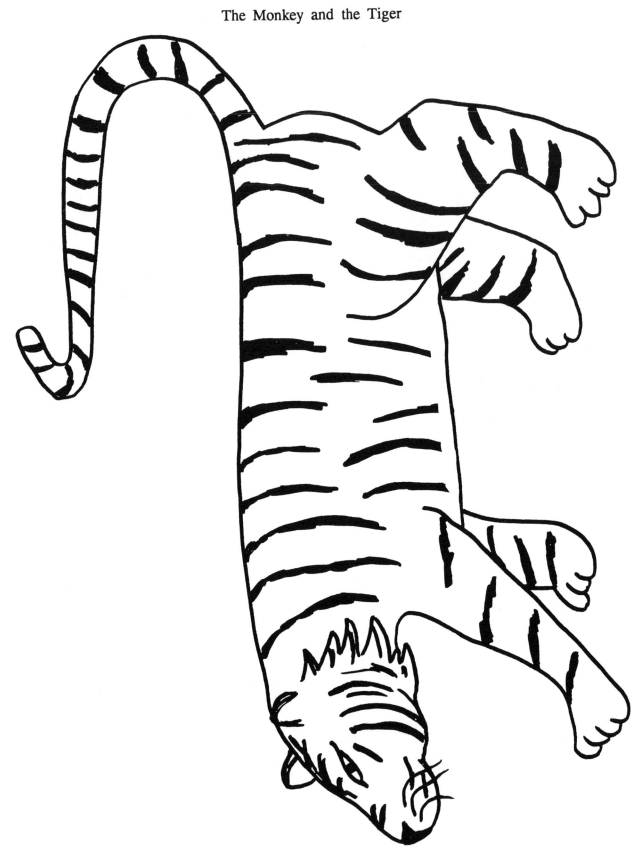

The Monkey And The Tiger

The Monkey And The Tiger

24

(Traditional)

1. I know an old lady who swallowed a fly. I don't know why she swallowed a fly. Perhaps she'll die.

2. I know an old lady who swallowed a spider that wriggled and jiggled and tickled inside her. She swallowed the spider to catch the fly. But I don't know why she swallowed the fly. Perhaps she'll die.

3. I know an old lady who swallowed a bird. How absurd to a swallow a bird. She swallowed the bird to catch the spider. She swallowed the spider to catch the fly. But I don't know why she swallowed the fly. Perhaps she'll die.

4. I know and old lady who swallowed a cat. Imagine that, to swallow a cat! She swallowed the cat to catch the bird. She swallowed the bird to catch the spider. She swallowed the spider to catch the fly. But I don't know why she swallowed the fly. Perhaps she'll die.

5. I know an old lady who swallowed a dog. What a hog, to swallow a dog! She swallowed the dog to catch the cat. She swallowed the cat to catch the bird. She swallowed the bird to catch the spider. She swallowed the spider to catch the fly. But I don't know why she swallowed the fly. Perhaps she'll die.

6. I know an old lady who swallowed a goat. She just opened up her throat and swallowed the goat! She swallowed the goat to catch the dog. She swallowed the dog to catch the cat. She swallowed the cat to catch the bird. She swallowed the bird to catch the spider. She swallowed the spider to catch the fly. But I don't know why she swallowed the fly. Perhaps she'll die.

7. I know an old lady who swallowed a horse. SHE DIED, OF COURSE!

Directions

Cut out three strips of black felt using the stomach outline pattern. Glue the ends together to form a circle which will represent the old lady's stomach. The hands should be glued onto the sides of the stomach outline, the feet to the bottom, and the head, of course, to the top. Place each animal or bug in or near her mouth first, then after the word "swallowed" put them in her stomach.

Color Suggestions	*Materials*
Stomach outline and feet - black	felt squares:
Sleeves and collar - pink	1 back
Hair - grey	1 grey
Fly and spider - black	1 skin color
Bird - red	A small amount of:
Cat - white	pink
Dog - brown	white
Goat - white	red
Horse - grey	brown
	googly eyes

26

Stomach out line

hands

Feet

28

The Old Lady Who Swallowed a Fly

29

THE PRINCESS AND THE PEA   Preschool - 2nd Grade
(Hans Christian Andersen)

There was once a prince, and he wanted a princess, but she must be a real princess. He traveled all over the world to find one, but there was always something wrong. There were plenty of princesses, but as to whether they were real princesses he had great difficulty in discovering. There was always something which was not quite right about them. So at last he had to come home again, and he was very sad because he wanted a real princess so badly.

One night there was a terrible storm. There was thunder and lightning and the rain poured down.

In the middle of the storm somebody knocked at the castle door and the old king himself went to answer it.

It was a princess and she was very cold and wet from the storm.

"Well, we shall soon see if she is a real princess," thought the old queen. Then she went into the bedroom and laid a single pea underneath the mattress that the princess was to sleep on. So the princess went to bed and was not able to sleep all night.

In the morning the king and queen asked her, "Did you sleep well?" "Oh, terribly badly!" said the princess. "I hardly closed my eyes the whole night. Heaven knows what was in the bed. I seemed to be lying on something very hard. It was terrible!"

The next night the queen decided to try another test. She piled many, many feather mattresses on top of the bed and left the pea underneath them. So the princess went to bed and again was not able to sleep all night.

The next morning the king and queen noticed that the princess looked very tired and they asked her, "Did you sleep well?" "Oh, absolutely terribly!" said the princess. "My whole body is black and blue this morning. I had an awful night!"

They saw at once that she must be a real princess when she had felt the pea through all those mattresses. Nobody but a real princess could have such delicate skin.

So the prince took her to be his wife, for now he was sure that he had found a real princess.

As for the pea, they put it in a museum and, unless someone has taken it, it's there still.

Directions

Start the story with the prince on the flannel board. Next, add the king, princess, and queen in succession according to the story. When the princess goes to bed remove the other figures and place the princess in bed while describing how uncomfortable she is. Do the same the next night, adding the extra mattresses (make several with the pattern). End the story with all the figures on the flannel board and put the wedding gown on the princess.

Color Suggestions

King's robe - purple, cotton trim
Queen - gold, purple
Prince - white shirt, tan pants,
   black boots, red cape
Princess - pink or yellow
Mattresses - multiple colors

Materials

felt squares:
2 purple
1 gold or yellow
1 white
1 red
1 black
1 pink
1 skin color

sequins
beads
cotton

mattress

33

The Princess and the Pea

36

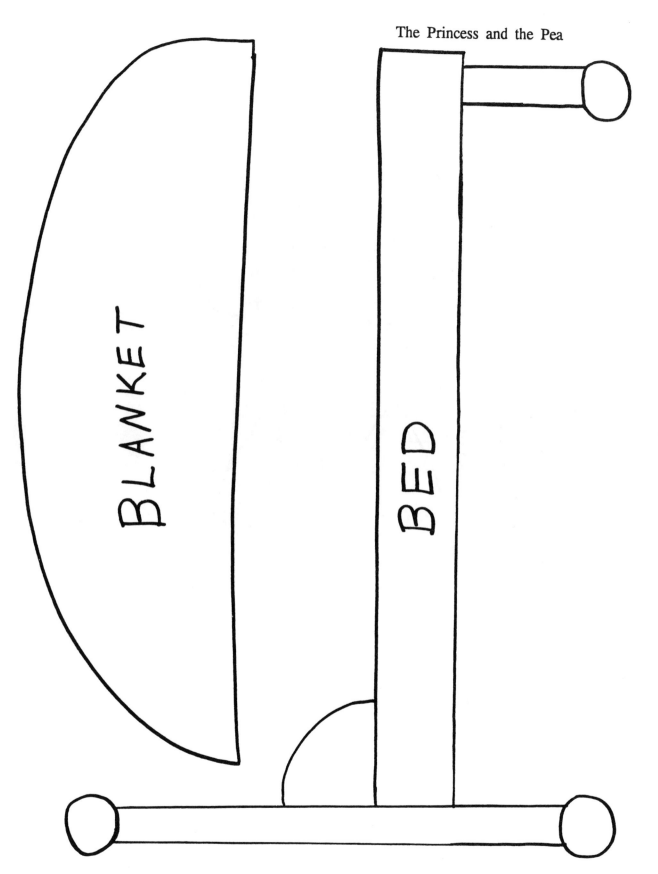

BLANKET

BED

cut
out

(An English Tale)

The cat and the mouse played in the malt-house. The cat bit the mouse's tail off. "Please, cat, give me my tail." "No," said the cat, "I'll not give you your tail, till you go to the cow, and fetch me some milk."

First she leapt and then she ran,
Till she came to the cow, and thus began:

"Please, cow, give me milk, that I may give cat milk, that cat may give me my own tail again." "No," said the cow, "I will give you no milk, till you go to the farmer, and get me some hay."

First she leapt and then she ran,
Till she came to the farmer, and thus began:

"Please, Farmer, give me hay, that I may give cow hay, that cow may give me milk, that I may give cat milk, that cat may give me my own tail again." "No," said the farmer, "I'll give you no hay, till you go to the butcher and fetch me some meat."

First she leapt and then she ran,
Till she came to the butcher, and thus began:

"Please, Butcher, give me meat, that I may give farmer meat, that farmer may give me hay, that I may give cow hay, that cow may give me milk, that I may give cat milk, that cat may give me my own tail again." "No," said the butcher, "I'll give you no meat, till you go to the baker and fetch me some bread."

First she leapt and then she ran,
Till she came to the baker, and thus began:

"Please, Baker, give me bread, that I may give butcher bread, that butcher may give me meat, that I may give farmer meat, that farmer may give me hay, that I may give cow hay, that cow may give me milk, that I may give cat milk, that cat may give me my own tail again."

"Yes," said the baker, "I'll give you some bread,
But if you eat my meal, I'll cut off your head."

Then the baker gave mouse bread, and mouse gave butcher bread, and butcher gave mouse meat, and mouse gave farmer meat, and farmer gave mouse hay, and mouse gave cow hay, and cow gave mouse milk, and mouse gave cat milk, and cat gave mouse her own tail again!

Draw a face and other details on both sides of the mouse. He will face left and right at different times in the story.

Place the cat and mouse on the center of the flannel board. Remove the mouse's tail and place it on the cat's mouth. On "she came to the cow" put the cow on the lower left corner of the flannel board and move the mouse next to it. Do the same with the farmer, butcher, and baker, putting them on the remaining three corners, clockwise, at the appropriate times. Give each item to the mouse and then to the butcher, farmer, cow, and cat and then, finally, put the mouse's tail back on.

Color Suggestions

Mouse - light brown
Cat - grey or white
Cow - black and white

Materials

felt squares:
2 white
1 grey
1 skin color
1 brown
A small amount of:
light brown
yellow, red
green, black

The Cat and the Mouse

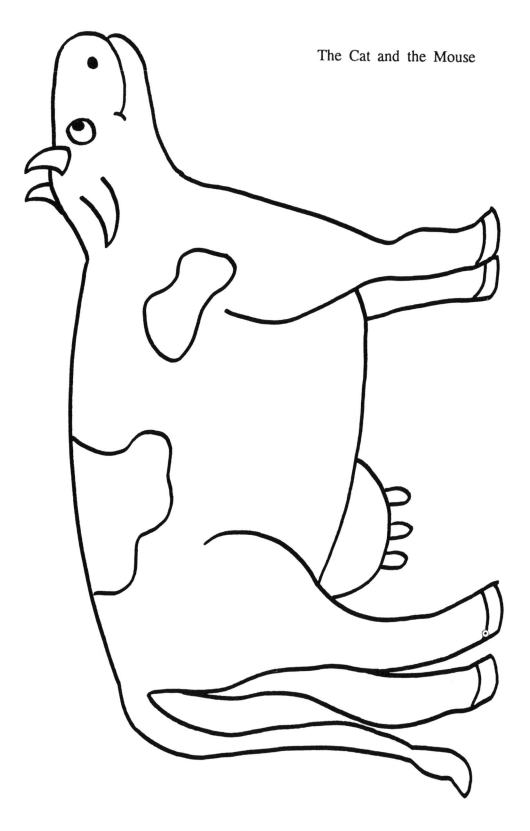

42

The Cat and the Mouse

bread

milk

meat

hay

FIVE IN THE BED

(Traditional)

1.   There were five in the bed, and the little one said, "Roll over, roll over." So they all rolled over, and one fell out;

2.   There were four in the bed ...

3.   There were three in the bed ...

4.   There were two in the bed ...

5.   There was one in the bed, and the little one said, "Good Night!"

Directions

Put all the children on the bed. Move each figure a little to the right on "roll over" and the one on the end will, of course, fall out. Do this until only the "little one" is left.

Color Suggestions

Mattress - white
Head board and
Foot board - tan
Pajamas - yellow, pink
green, red, blue

Materials

felt squares:
1 white, 1 tan
A small amount of: yellow, pink, green,
red, blue, skin color (cream, tan or brown)

Five in the Bed

46

Five in the Bed

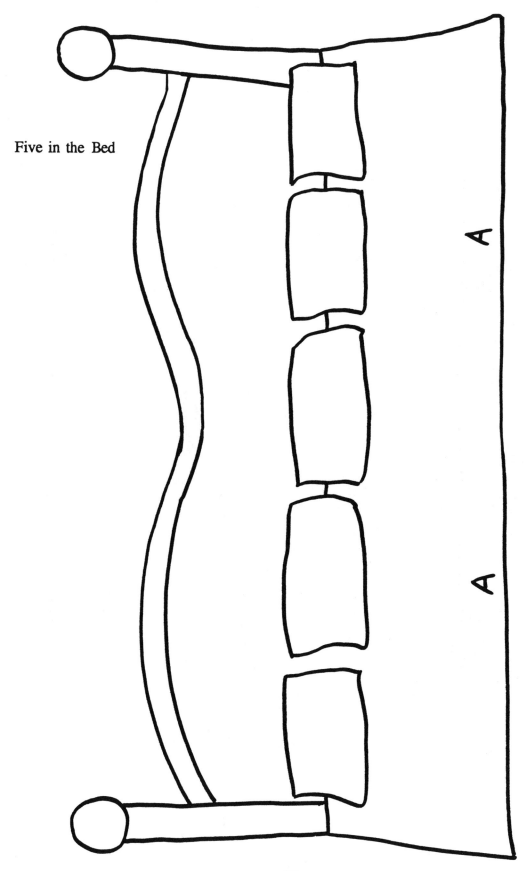

A

A

Five in the Bed

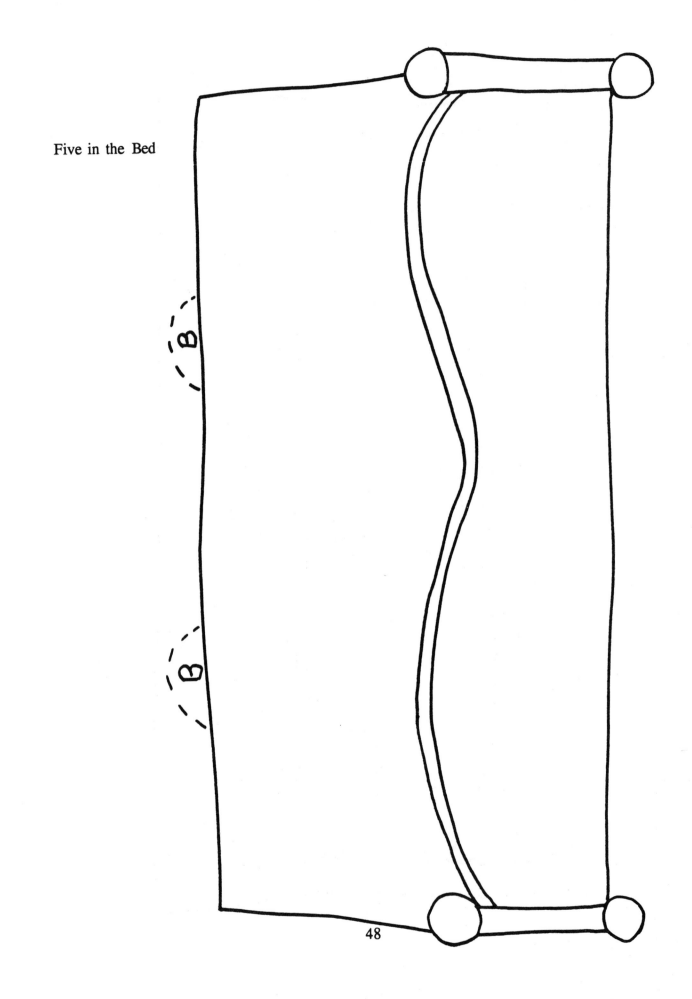

48

MY BIG PURPLE HAT

(by Diane Sherman Briggs)

I like to wear my big purple hat. I never know when it will come in handy. I'm going on a picnic in the meadow and my big purple hat will keep the sun out of my eyes.

Hey, is that a rain cloud? Oh, no, it's starting to rain. But I don't need to worry. My big purple hat will keep me dry.

Look, here comes a little white rabbit to get out of the rain under my big purple hat, and a pretty red bird who sits on my shoulder, and a cute little field mouse, and a little spotted fawn. And, look, here comes a pink butterfly to get out of the rain under my big purple hat.

But that's not all. Along comes a big fuzzy bear who is too tall to get under my big purple hat. So I put the hat on him and we all stay dry under my big purple hat.

Suddenly, there is a gust of wind that blows my big purple hat away. The pretty red bird flies away to get it. We all get a little wet, but the rain is beginning to stop. Here comes the red bird with my hat. And, look, the sun is coming out. Let's all go find a nice place to have a picnic.

There goes the big fuzzy bear, and the pink butterfly, and the little spotted fawn, and the cute little field mouse, and the pretty red bird, and the little white rabbit.

I sure am glad I wore my big purple hat.

Directions

To make the rain cloud, cut out two layers of felt and glue tinsel between the layers. Place the animals on the flannel board in succession as they appear in the story. Remove them in reverse order at the end of the story.

Color Suggestions	*Materials*
Girl - yellow dress	felt squares:
Rabbit - white	1 tan
Bird - red	1 purple
Mouse - tan	1 dark brown
Fawn - tan	1 yellow
Butterfly - pink	A small amount of:
Hat - purple	white, red
Bear - dark brown	pink, skin color

49

My Big Purple Hat

My Big Purple Hat

52

My Big Purple Hat

My Big Purple Hat

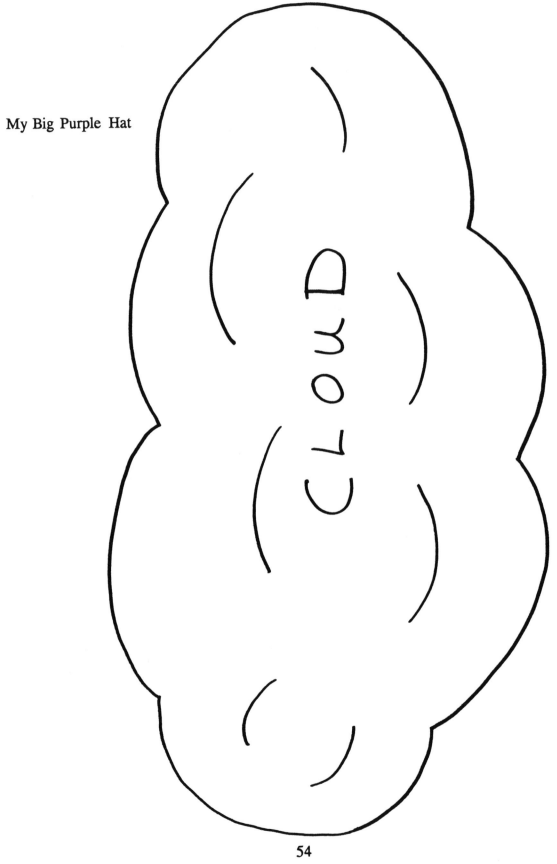

CLOUD

My Big Purple Hat

55

(Author Unknown)

Five little fishes swimming in a pool
First one said, "This pool is cool."
Second one said, "This pool is deep."
Third one said, "I think I'll sleep."
Fourth one said, "Let's swim and dip."
Fifth one said, "I see a ship."
The fisherman's line went splish, splish, splash!
And away the five little fishes dashed.

Directions

As you recite the rhyme place each fish on the flannel board one at a time. After "I see a ship," put the fisherman on the flannel board. At the end of the rhyme remove all the fish. For fun have the children imitate the way fish move their mouths.

Color Suggestions

Fish - green, orange
  grey, pink, yellow
Fisherman - yellow rain coat
  and hat
Boat - grey

Materials

felt squares:
yellow, grey
A small amount of: green, orange, grey, pink

small piece of string for fishing pole
googly eyes

56

Five Little Fishes

Five Little Fishes

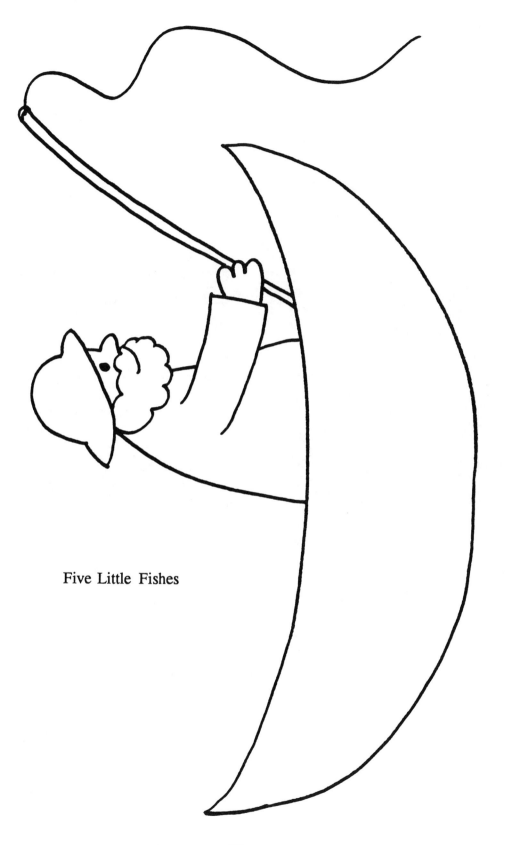

Five Little Fishes

DOWN ON GRANDPA'S FARM

Toddler - 2nd Grade

(Traditional)

1. Oh, we're on our way, we're on our way, on our way to Grandpa's farm. We're on our way, we're on our way, on our way to Grandpa's farm. Down on Grandpa's farm there is a big brown cow, down on Grandpa's farm there is a big brown cow. The cow, she makes a sound like this: Moo! The cow she makes a sound like this: Moo!

2. Down on Grandpa's farm there is a little red hen...

3. Down on Grandpa's farm there is a little white sheep...

4. Down on Grandpa's farm there is a big black dog...

5. Down on Grandpa's farm there is a big brown horse...

Directions

Add the animals to the flannel board as you sing. You might want to use these figures for "Old McDonald" as well, adding a few more animals of your own design.

Materials

felt squares:
2 brown
1 white
1 black
A small amount of:
red, skin color

60

Down on Grandpa's Farm

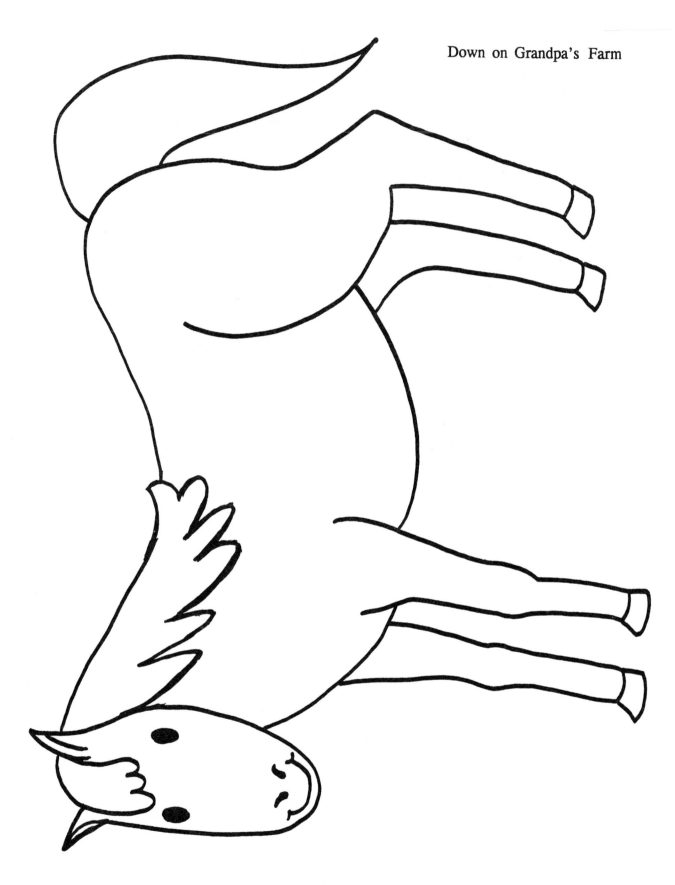

Down on Grandpa's Farm

64

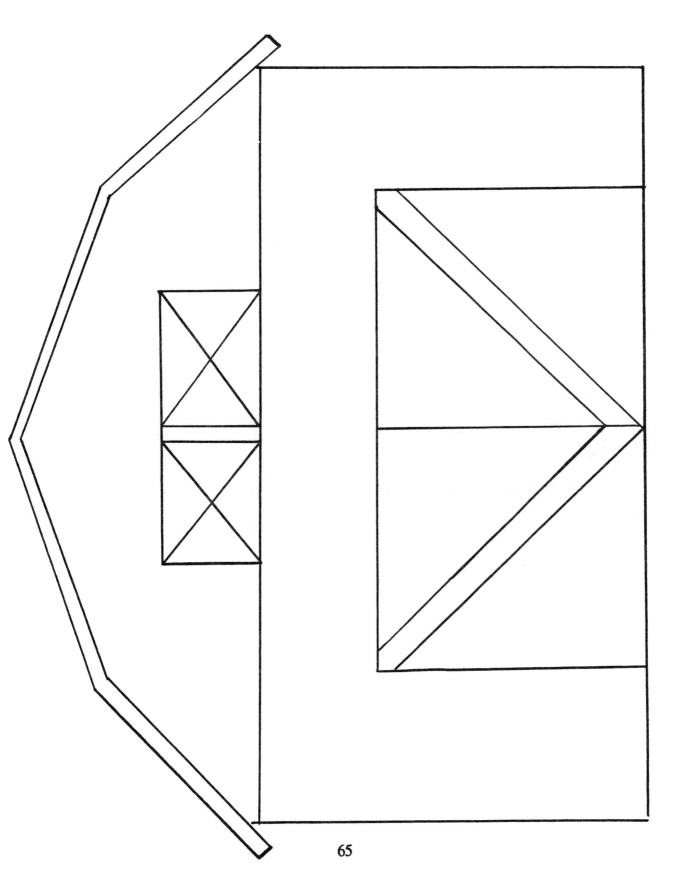

THE THREE BILLY GOATS GRUFF   Toddler - 2nd Grade
(A Norwegian Tale)

Once upon a time there were three billy goats and their name was Gruff. One day they found that they had eaten all the grass on their hillside and they wanted to go up to the green hillside across the river to make themselves fat. There was a bridge over the river they had to cross, and under the bridge lived an ugly troll with sharp teeth and a nose as long as a cucumber.

First of all came the youngest Billy Goat Gruff to cross the bridge. "Trip, trap, trip, trap" went the bridge.

"Who's that tripping over my bridge?!" roared the troll.

"Oh, it is only I, the tiniest Billy Goat Gruff, and I'm going up to the hillside to make myself fat."

"Now, I'm coming to eat you up!" yelled the troll.

"Oh, no! Don't eat me. I'm too little, that I am. Wait a bit until the second Billy Goat Gruff comes. He's much bigger and would make a better meal for you."

"Very well! Be off with you," said the troll.

A little while later came the second Billy Goat Gruff to cross the bridge. "Trip, trap! Trip, trap! Trip, trap!" went the bridge.

"Who's that tripping over my bridge?!" roared the troll.

"It is I, the second Billy Goat Gruff, and I'm going up to the hillside to make myself fat."

"Now, I'm coming to eat you up!" yelled the troll.

"Oh, no! Don't eat me. Wait a little until the big Billy Goat Gruff comes. He's much bigger and juicier and has more meat on his bones," said the billy goat.

"Very, well! Be off with you," said the troll.

Just then, up came the big Billy Goat Gruff. "TRIP, TRAP! TRIP, TRAP! TRIP, TRAP!" went the bridge.

"Who's that tramping over my bridge?!" roared the troll.

"It is I! The big Billy Goat Gruff!"

"Now, I'm coming to eat you up!" yelled the troll.

"Well, come along! And I'll butt you right off this bridge," said the billy goat.

And that's just what the billy goat did. He flew at the troll and tossed him into the river. Then he went up to the hillside.

If there is still grass on that hillside the three billy goats are there still, and so snip, snap, snout, this tale's told out.

Directions

Make two hills with the pattern. Put the two hills, with the bridge between them, on the flannel board before you begin the story. Start with the billy goats on the left hill. Place the troll under the bridge and bring him up onto the bridge to meet each billy goat as they cross. Put him back under the bridge each time. At the end of the story have the big goat butt him off the bridge and place the troll on the lower right corner of the flannel board on his back.

Color Suggestions	Materials
Goats - white	felt squares:
Horns and hoofs - tan	1 white
Hills - 1 brown, 1 green	1 purple
Bridge - yellow	1 brown
Troll - purple pants	1 green
green body	1 yellow
	A small amount of:
	tan
	googly eyes

The Three Billy Goats Gruff

The Three Billy Goats Gruff

BRIDGE

The Three Billy Goats Gruff

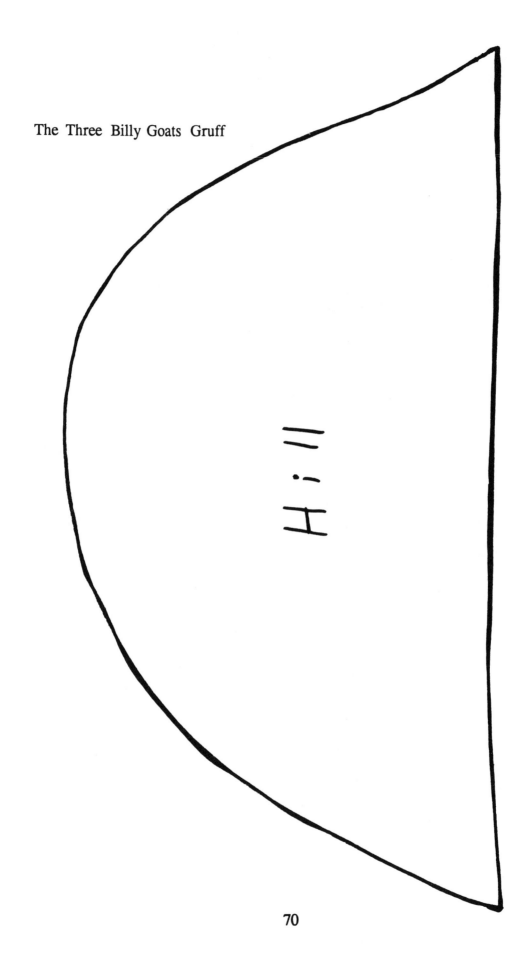

Hill

OVER IN THE MEADOW

Toddler - 2nd Grade

(Traditional)

1. Over in the meadow in the sand in the sun lived an old mother turtle and her little turtle one. "Hide!" said the mother. "I hide!" said the one. So she hid all day in the sand and the sun.

2. Over in the meadow in a nest built of sticks lived a pretty mother bird and her little birds six. "Sing!" said the mother. "We sing!" said the six. So they sang all day in their nest made of sticks.

3. Over in the meadow in the shade of the tree was a pink mother pig and her little piggies three. "Oink!" said the mother. "We oink!" said the three. So they oinked all day in the shade of the tree.

4. Over in the meadow in the pond so blue lived a daddy salamander and his little ones two. "Crawl!" said the daddy "We crawl!" said the two. So they crawled all day around the pond so blue.

5. Over in the meadow, in a sly little den lived an old mother spider, and her little spiders ten. "Spin!" said the mother, "We spin!" said the ten. So they spun lacy webs in their sly little den.

Directions

As you sing each verse place the appropriate animals on the flannel board. On "hide" fold the turtles' heads under their shells. You will need to make three piglets and two baby salamanders. Use the tree pattern from "Three Little Monkeys" (pp. 86-87).

Add verses of your own if you prefer.

Color Suggestions

Turtles - green
Birds - blue
Salamanders - orange
Pigs - pink
Spiders - black

Materials

felt squares:
2 green
1 black
1 brown
1 pink
1 orange
1 blue

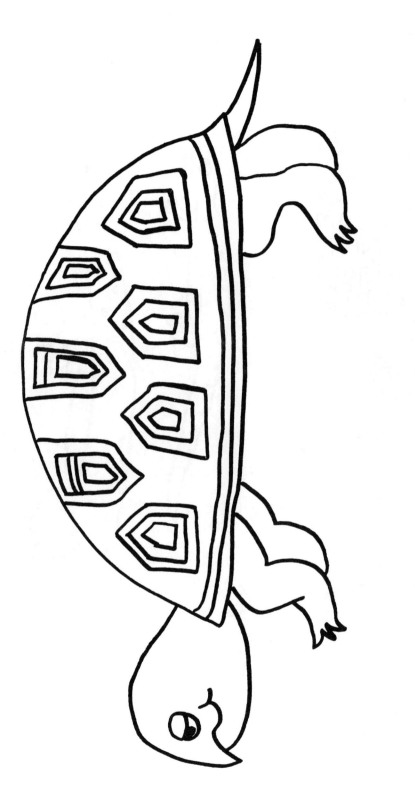

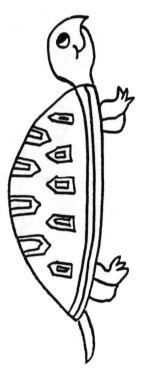

(An English Tale)

Once there was a little old woman and a little old man who lived all alone in a little cottage. They had always wanted to have children and they never did. So one day, the little old woman made a little boy out of gingerbread. She gave him two raisin eyes, a pink sugar nose, a licorice mouth, and a chocolate hat, and popped him into the oven to bake. When the baking was done she opened up the oven and out jumped the gingerbread boy. Away he ran out the door and down the road.

The little old woman and the little old man chased him down the road as fast as they could, but they couldn't catch him and he called back at them, "Run! Run! As fast as you can! You can't catch me, I'm the Gingerbread Man!"

The Gingerbread Boy ran on and on down the road until he came upon a fat pink pig. "Come over here, little Gingerbread Boy," said the pig. "You look delicious."

The Gingerbread Boy just laughed and said, "I've run away from the little old woman and the little old man, and I can run away from you, I can! So run! Run! As fast as you can! You can't catch me, I'm the Gingerbread Man!"

And the pig couldn't catch him.

The Gingerbread Boy ran on and on down the road until he came upon a cow. "Moo," said the cow. "Come closer, little Gingerbread Boy, so I can take a bite."

"Oh no!" said the Gingerbread Boy. "I've run away from the little old woman and the little old man and the pig, and I can run away from you, I can! So run! Run! As fast as you can! You can't catch me, I'm the Gingerbread Man!"

And the cow couldn't catch him.

On and on the Gingerbread Boy ran down the road until he came upon a bear. When the bear smelled the Gingerbread Boy he said, "Little Gingerbread Boy, please stop. I would like to eat you."

"Oh, no!" said the Gingerbread Boy. "I've run away from the little old woman and the little old man, a pig, and a cow, and I can run away from you, I can. So run! Run! As fast as you can! You can't catch me, I'm the Gingerbread Man!"

And the bear couldn't catch him. On down the road the Gingerbread Boy ran, as fast as ever.

Next, the Gingerbread Boy came upon a fox. "Come here, little Gingerbread Boy," said the fox.

And the Gingerbread Boy said, "Oh, no! I've run away from the little old woman and the little old man and ..."

"What?" said the fox. "I can hardly hear you. Come closer."

So the Gingerbread Boy came a little closer and said, "I've run away from the little old woman ..."

"What?" said the fox. "Come a little closer. I still can't hear you."

So the Gingerbread Boy took a few more steps towards the fox and yelled in his ear, "I said, I've run away from the ..." And chomp, chomp, the fox ate him.

And that was the end of the Gingerbread Boy.

Directions

Cut the door of the stove so that it opens. At the beginning of the story place the old woman and the old man next to the stove. Next put the Gingerbread Boy in the stove.

When he jumps out and runs away, remove the stove and the old woman and old man. Place the rest of the animals on the flannel board at the proper times and remove them when the Gingerbread Boy runs away. Move the Gingerbread Boy a little closer to the fox each time the fox says "Come closer". When the fox eats him, snatch him quickly off the flannel board.

Color Suggestions	*Materials*
Gingerbread Boy - tan	felt squares:
Pig - pink	1 tan
Cow - brown and white	1 pink
Bear - dark brown	1 brown
Fox - orange and white	1 white
Old woman - pink dress	1 orange
Old man - brown and green	1 green
	A small amount of:
	skin color

The Gingerbread Boy

The Gingerbread Boy

80

The Gingerbread Boy

(Fingerplay)

Three little monkeys swinging in a tree
(hold up three fingers and move side to side)

Teasing Mr. Crocodile, "You can't catch me!"
(wag one finger)

Along comes crocodile quiet as can be
(palms together making waving motion)

And SNAP!
(snap palms together)

Two little monkeys...(repeat above)

One little monkey... (repeat above and change last line)

SNAP! Ha, ha, you missed me!

Directions

Make three monkeys with the pattern. Use different colors if you prefer. Set the characters up on the flannel board before you start the fingerplay. After each "snap" move the crocodile toward one of the monkeys to "snap" him off the tree. Remove the monkey from the flannel board and put the crocodile back under the tree. To prolong the fun this can also be done with five monkeys or more.

Color Suggestions

Monkeys - tan, brown, orange
Crocodile - green

Materials

felt squares:
1 brown
2 green
A small amount of:
tan, orange

Three Little Monkeys

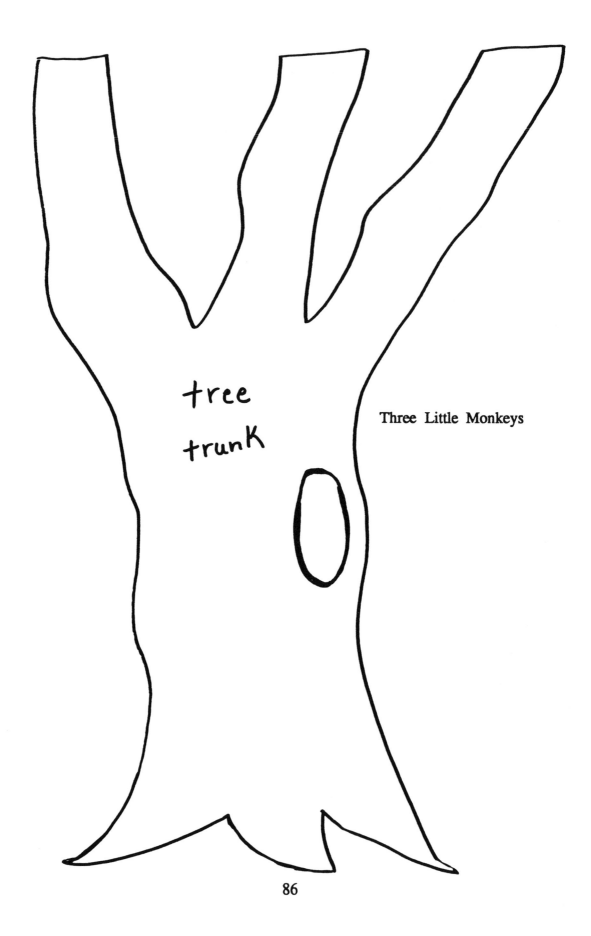

tree
trunk

Three Little Monkeys

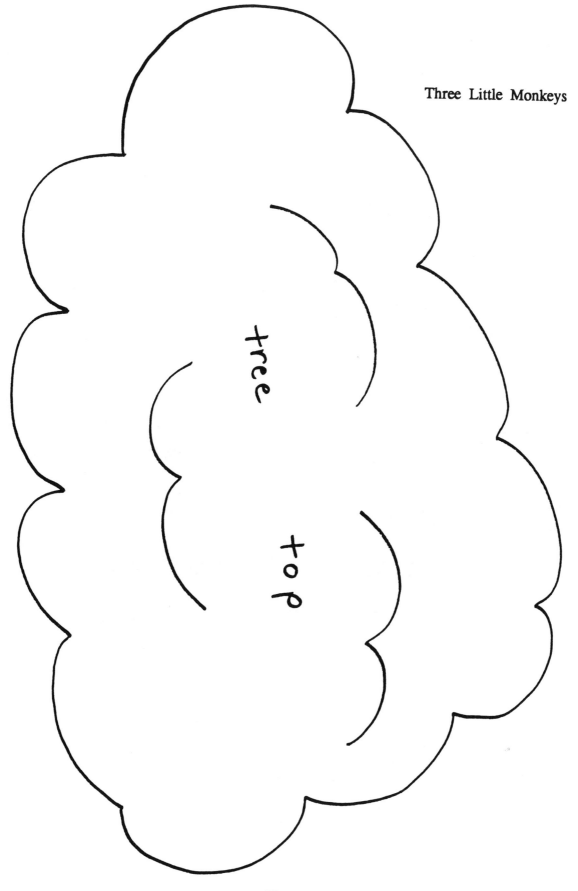

Three Little Monkeys

tree

top

87

LITTLE ROBIN REDBREAST

(Mother Goose)

Little Robin Redbreast sat upon a tree,
Up went the Pussy-Cat, and down went he,
Down came Pussy-Cat, away Robin ran;
Says little Robin Redbreast: "Catch me if you can!"
Little Robin Redbreast jumped upon a spade,
Pussy-Cat jumped after him, and then he was afraid;
Little Robin chirped and sang, and what did Pussy say?
Pussy-Cat said: "Mew, mew, mew," and Robin flew away.

Directions

Use the tree pattern from "Three Little Monkeys" (pp. 86-87). Move the figures on the flannel board according to the action in the rhyme.

Color Suggestions

Robin - brown and red/orange
Cat - white
Spade - grey with a brown handle

Materials

felt squares:
1 brown
1 green
A small amount of:
red/orange, yellow,
white, grey

STONE SOUP
(A Russian Tale)

Once there was an old woman who set out on a journey to visit a friend who lived far away. On her way she became tired and hungry and knocked on the door of the first house she came to. An old man answered the door and said, "Yes, what can I do for you?"

The old woman answered, "Sir, could you help me? I'm tired and hungry. Could you perhaps spare a bit of food?" And the old man said, "Oh, no! I have no food to give you. I barely have enough for myself!" And the old woman said, "But I can show you how to make soup from a stone." "Soup from a stone! I never heard of such a thing!" said the old man. But he was curious and he let the old woman in. Then the old man brought a potful of water and put it over the fire so the old woman could make the soup. All the while he was thinking, "If I could learn how to make soup from a stone I would never go hungry."

The old woman pulled a stone from her pocket and dropped it in the pot -- KERPLUNK-- and said, "Well, now, we'll just let that simmer a while and, oh, by the way, do you have any salt?" The old man was grumpy about it but he brought the salt. After a while the old woman said, "Oh, do you know what would make this soup even better? Some potatoes and an onion." The old man grumbled again but he brought the potatoes and onion. Now the soup was beginning to smell especially good and after it simmered a while longer the old woman said, "This soup would be absolutely excellent if only we had some carrots and a bit of meat." The old man didn't complain this time because the soup smelled so good. The old woman put the carrots and meat into the pot and it simmered for a while more and finally the soup was ready.

The old woman and the old man ate large bowls of soup and said it was the most wonderfully delicious soup they had ever tasted. And a fine soup it was and all from a stone.

Directions

Place the vegetables and meat on the top of the soup pot as they are added. On "finally the soup was ready" replace the fire and pot with the table.

Color Suggestions	*Materials*
Pot - gray	felt squares:
Fire - yellow and orange	1 gray, 1 brown, 1 yellow
Old man - red shirt	A small amount of:
brown pants	pink, orange, white
Old woman - pink and yellow	red, skin color

Stone Soup

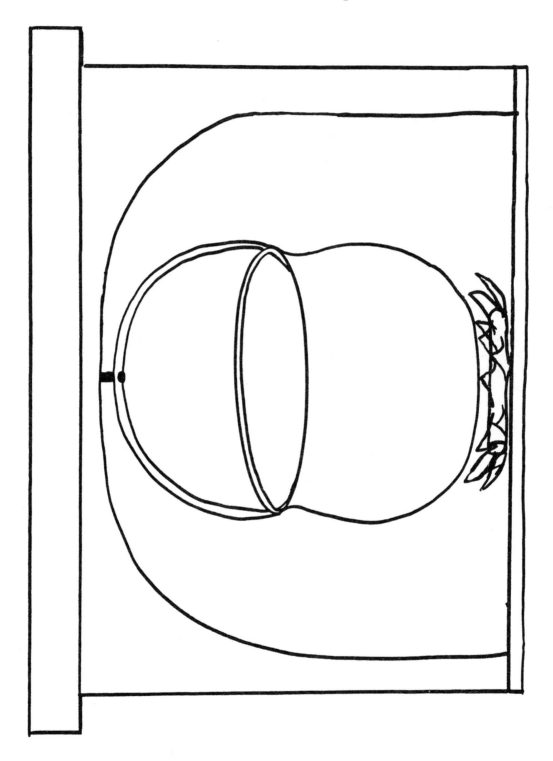

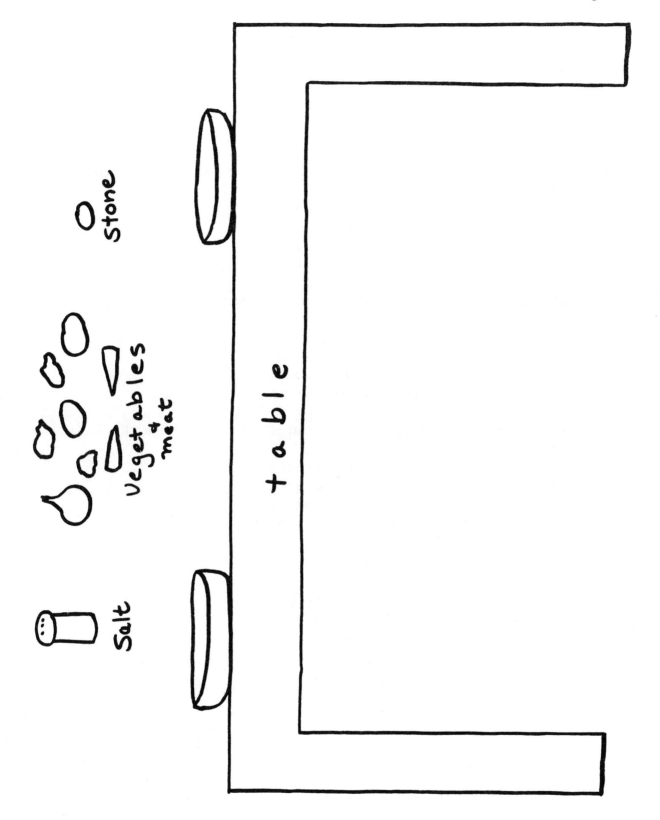

Stone

Salt

Vegetables & meat

table

93

THE STRANGE VISITOR

(An English Tale)

An old woman was sitting at her spinning wheel one night.

> And still she sat
> And still she spun
> And still she waited
> For someone to come in.

Then... in came a pair of big, big feet, and sat themselves down on the cold, cold floor.

> And still she sat
> And still she spun
> And still she waited
> For someone to come in.

Then... in came a pair of thin, thin legs, and sat down on the big, big feet.

> And still she sat
> And still she spun
> And still she waited
> For someone to come in.

Then... in came a pair of huge, huge hips, and sat down on the thin, thin legs.

> And still she sat
> And still she spun
> And still she waited
> For someone to come in.

Then... in came a wee, wee waist, and sat down on the huge, huge hips.

> And still she sat
> And still she spun
> And still she waited
> For someone to come in.

Then... in came a broad, broad chest, and sat down on the wee, wee waist.

> And still she sat
> And still she spun
> And still she waited
> For someone to come in.

Then... in came a pair of long, long arms, and sat down on the broad, broad chest.

And still she sat
And still she spun
And still she waited
For someone to come in.

Then... in came a pair of large, large hands, and sat down on the long, long arms. "How strange," said the woman, "to see such large, large hands on those long, long arms on that broad, broad chest on that wee, wee waist on those huge, huge hips on those thin, thin legs on those big, big feet on this cold, cold floor."

But, still she sat
And still she spun
And still she waited
For someone to come in.

Then... in rolled a BIG, BIG Head! And sat down on the broad, broad chest. "OOH MY!!" said the woman. "How did you get such big, big feet?" "Much walking, much walking." "How did you get such thin, thin legs?" "Aih-h-h!-late and wee-e-e-moul."* "How did you get such huge, huge hips?" "Much sitting, much sitting." "How did you get such a wee, wee waist?" "Aih-h-h!-late and wee-e-e-moul." "How did you get such a broad, broad chest?" "Much hard work, much hard work." "How did you get such long, long arms?" "Aih-h-h!-late and wee-e-e-moul." "How did you get such large, large hands?" "With carrying broom, with carrying broom." "How did you get such a BIG, BIG Head?!" "It's a pumpkinshell! It's a pumpkinshell!" "What did you come for?" "To get you!!"

Directions

After telling this story you may want to distribute the bones to your audience and let them help you tell it again.

Color Suggestions

Use some calico cloth
for the woman's dress
Hair - grey

Materials

felt squares:
2 white
1 orange
1 brown
A small amount of:
grey, skin color

calico cloth

* Up late and little food.

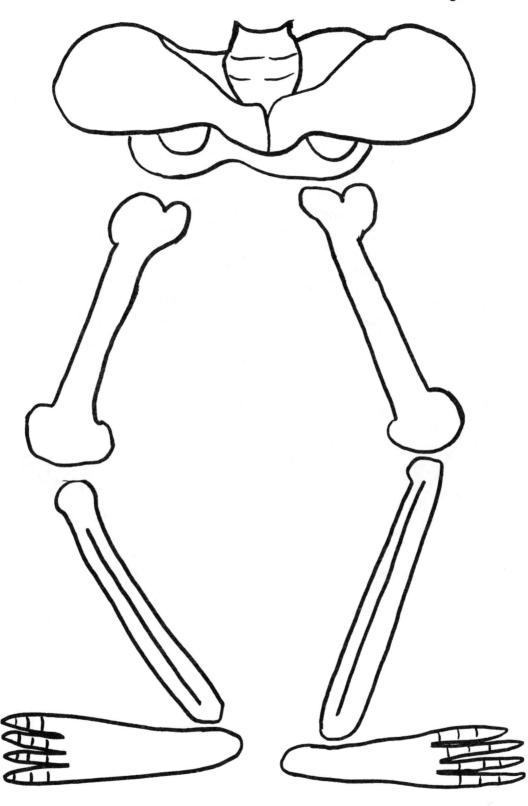

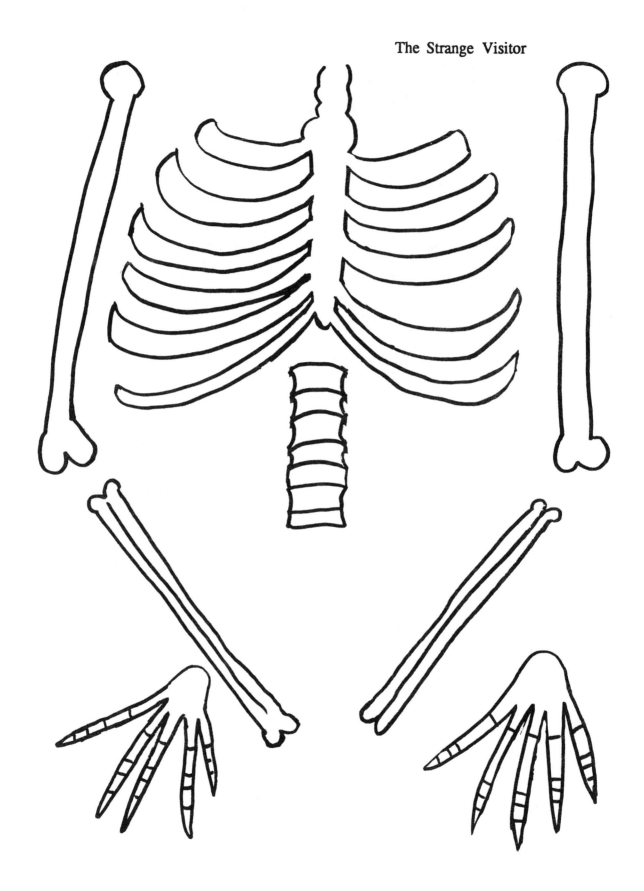

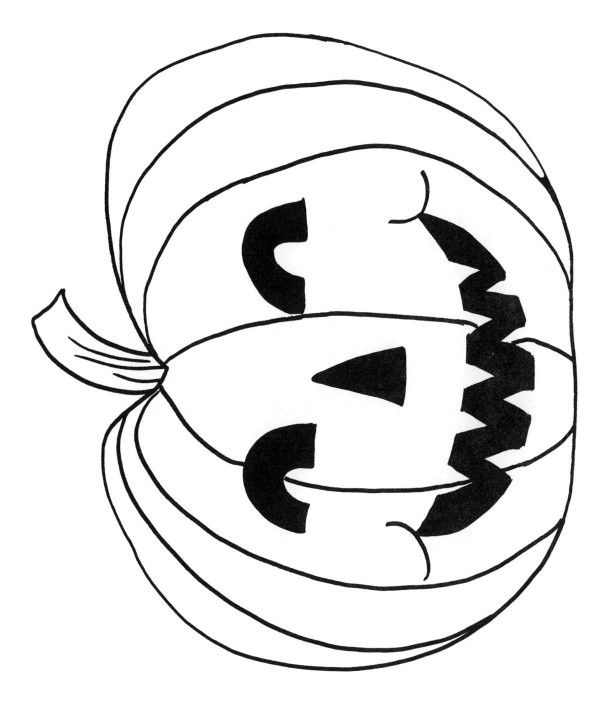

One day a little girl was playing outside of the house where she lived with her papa. The papa did not want his little daughter to run into the forest, where there were wolves. He told his little daughter to never, on no account, leave their yard alone. The little girl said, "Oh, I won't, papa."

One morning the little girl's papa had to go away for something. The little girl saw some beautiful flowers a little ways off from the house and she wanted to go and pick some of them. So out she went away from the house and near to the forest to pick the flowers. The flowers smelled sweet and she wanted to pick more and more of them to make a pretty bunch for her vase on the table. The whole time she was doing this she was singing a sweet song: "Tray-bla, tray-bla, cum qua, kimo."

All of a sudden she heard a noise. She looked up and saw a great big gunny wolf and the wolf said to her, "Sing that sweetest, goodest song again."

So the little girl sang it again. "Tray-bla, tray-bla, cum qua, kimo." The gunny wolf starts to close his eyes and pit-a-pat, pit-a-pat, pit-a-pat, pit-a-pat, the little girl tiptoes back toward her house.

But she hears a noise behind her and there's the wolf and he says, "Did you move?" The little girl says, "I no move. What occasion have I to move?"

"Well, sing that sweet little, good little song again." The little girl sings it: "Tray-bla, tray-bla, cum qua kimo."

And the wolf starts to fall asleep again. The little girl starts to tiptoe some more. Pit-a-pat, pit-a-pat, pit-a-pat.

But very soon she hears a growl behind her and there's the wolf again and he says, "I think you moved."

The little girl says, "I no move. What occasion have I to move?"

So the wolf says, "Sing that sweet little, good little song again."

The little girl begins: "Tray-bla, tray-bla, cum qua kimo."

The wolf falls asleep. The little girl tiptoes, pit-a-pat, pit-a-pat, and she is getting very close to her house now.

There's the wolf behind her and he says, "You moved." The little girl says, "Oh, no, I no move."

"Well then, sing that sweetest, goodest song again," says the gunny wolf. So she starts: "Tray-bla, tray-bla ..." The gunny wolf falls asleep.

This time the little girl tiptoes all the way back to her house and slams the door behind her, right in the wolf's face. Now she was good and safe. The gunny wolf never did catch her.

Directions

Using the tree pattern from "Three Little Monkeys" (pp. 86-87), make two trees and put them on the right side of the flannel board. This will be the forest. Place the house on the left. Cut the door of the house so that it opens. As the little girl picks flowers place a few bunches on her arm. On "pit-a-pat" move the little girl closer to her house each time. At the end of the story put the little girl in her house and close the door. Have the children join in on the "pit-a-pats" and the song.

Color Suggestions	*Materials*
House - red and brown	felt squares:
Wolf - grey	1 red
Flowers - yellow	2 brown
red	2 green
purple	1 grey
Dress - pink	A small amount of:
white	yellow, purple,
	pink, white,
	skin color (medium brown)

ROOF

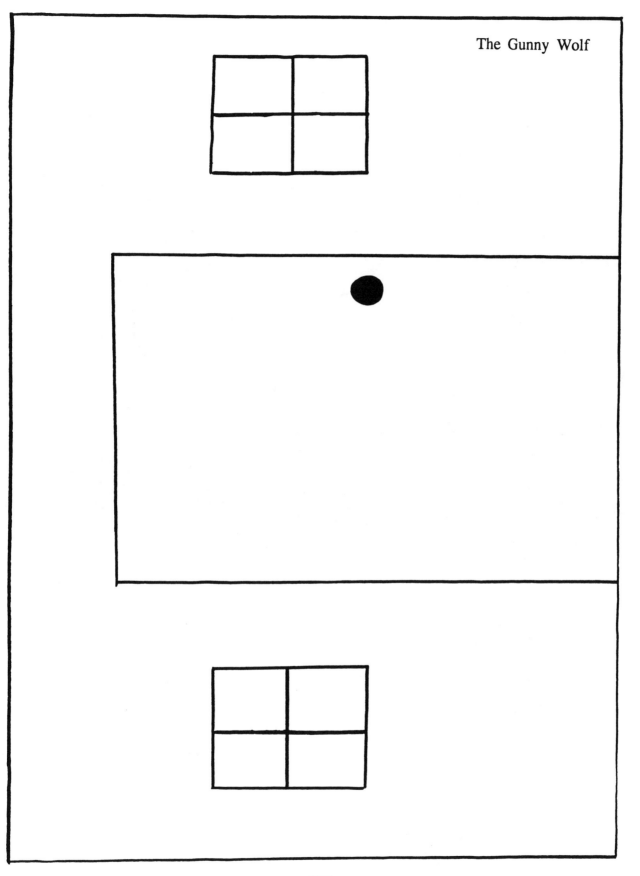

The Gunny Wolf

THE WELL OF THE WORLD'S END   Preschool - 3rd Grade
(An English Tale)

Once upon a time there was a girl who lived with her stepmother, who was a widow. The stepmother had no use for the girl and was very cruel to her. One day she sent her off to fill a sieve with water. She said, "Go fill it at the Well of the World's End and bring it home to me full, or woe betide you."

Well, the girl started off but she hadn't any idea how to find the Well of the World's End. On her way down the road she met a strange little old woman who told her how to get there. Finally she arrived at the Well of the World's End. But when she dipped the sieve into the cold, cold water, it all ran out again. The girl began to cry. Suddenly she heard a croaking voice and then she saw a big frog looking at her with goggle eyes. "What's the matter, dearie?" it said. "Oh, my stepmother sent me to fill the sieve with water and I can't fill it at all." "Well," said the frog, "if you promise me to do whatever I bid for a whole night long, I'll tell you how to fill it." The girl agreed and the frog said, "Stop it with moss and daub it with clay, and then it will carry the water away." Then the frog went into the Well of the World's End. So the girl did what the frog told her to do and got the water. Before she left, the frog popped his head out once more and said, "Remember your promise."

The girl returned to her home and that very evening at supper time there came a tap - tap - tapping at the door low down, and a voice cried out:

> Open the door, my honey, my heart
> Open the door, my own darling;
> Mind you the words that you and I spoke,
> down at the World's End Well.

Now the girl had to tell her stepmother about the frog. "Girls must keep their promises," said the stepmother, for she was glad the girl would have to obey a nasty frog. So the girl let the frog in. Then the frog said:

> Let me eat from your plate, my honey, my heart
> Give me some supper, my darling;
> Remember the words you and I spoke,
> Down at the World's End Well.

Although she didn't like it at all she let the frog eat from her plate. And when the frog finished, it said:

> Go with me to bed, my honey, my heart,
> Go with me to bed, my own darling;
> Mind you the words you spoke to me,
> Down by the cold well, so weary.

105

That, the girl did not want to do at all, till her stepmother said, "Do what you promised, girl. Girls must keep their promises. Do what you are bid, or out you go, you and your froggie."

So the girl took the frog with her to bed, and kept it as far away from her as she could. Well, just as the sun was starting to come up, what should the frog say but:

Give me a kiss, my honey, my heart,
Give me a kiss, my own darling;
Remember the promise you made to me,
Down by the cold well so weary.

At first the girl wouldn't do it. But when the frog said the words over again she did his bidding and in a flash there stood before her a handsome prince, who told her he had been enchanted by a wicked witch and that she had broken the spell. Then they went off together and were married and went to live in the castle of the king. They lived happily the rest of their lives.

Directions

The frog should be hidden under the well when it is placed on the flannel board. Pull the frog out of the well when he talks to the girl. When he eats off her plate place him on the table. At the end of the story snatch him quickly off the flannel board and replace him with the prince.

Color Suggestions	*Materials*
Girl's dress - white and blue	felt squares:
Stepmother's dress - grey	1 black
Well - grey and black	1 grey
Blanket - pink	1 green
Prince - red cape,	1 brown
white shirt, brown pants,	1 pink
black boots	1 white
	A small amount of:
	yellow, blue, skin color
	googly eyes for frog

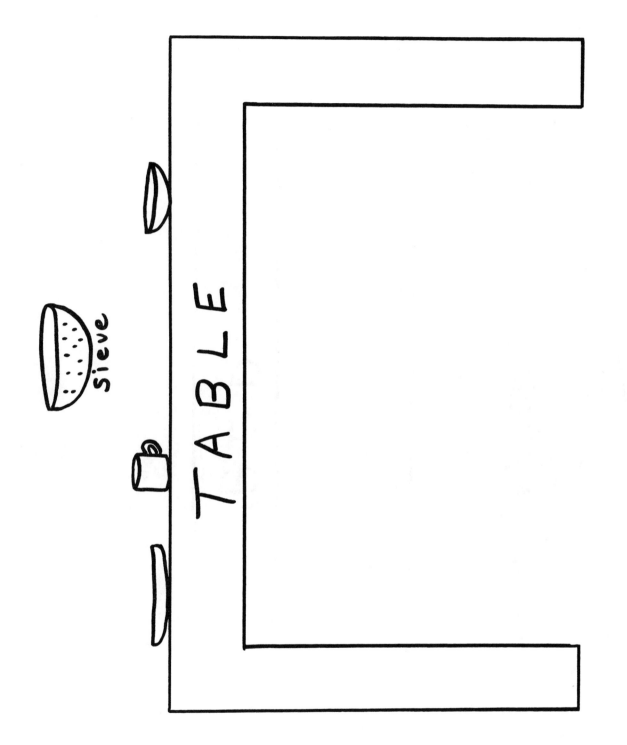

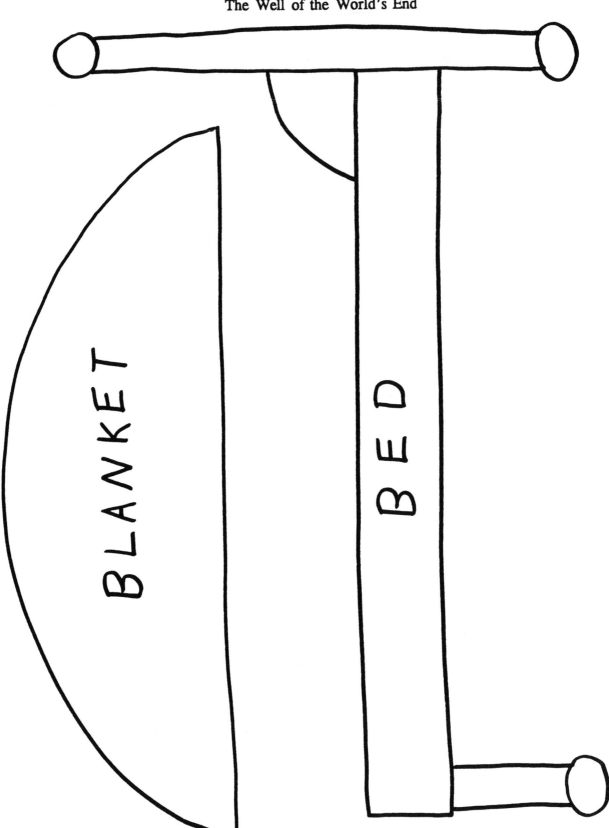

The Well of the World's End

111

HEY, DIDDLE, DIDDLE

(Mother Goose)

Hey, diddle, diddle
The cat and the fiddle,
The cow jumped over the moon;
The little dog laughed
To see such sport,
And the dish ran away with the spoon.

Color Suggestions

Cat - orange with stripes
Cow - brown and white
Dog - tan with dark brown spots
Dish - white
Spoon - grey
Moon - yellow

Materials

felt squares:
1 yellow
2 white
A small amount of:
orange, brown,
tan, grey, black

112

Hey, Diddle Diddle

113

Hey, Diddle Diddle

114

Hey, Diddle Diddle

115

FIVE FAT TURKEYS
(Traditional)

Five Fat Turkeys are we.
We slept all night in a tree.
When the cook came around
We couldn't be found.
So that's why we're here, you see.

FIVE FAT TURKEYS
(A Rhyme)

Five fat turkeys sitting on a fence
First one said, "I'm so immense."
Second one said, "I can gobble at you."
Third one said, "I can gobble too."
Fourth one said, "I can spread my tail."
Fifth one said, "Don't catch it on a nail."
A farmer came along and stopped to say: "Turkeys look best on Thanksgiving Day!"

Directions

Use the tree pattern from "Three Little Monkeys" (pp. 86-87). Start the song after placing the turkeys in the tree. On "When the cook came around" put the cook on the flannel board.

Before reciting the rhyme remove the turkeys from the tree and then place them on the fence one by one as you recite the rhyme. (Make a fence with strips of brown felt.)

116

Color Suggestions

Turkeys - light brown
with feathers glued on
Fence - brown

Materials

felt squares:
2 light brown
1 brown
1 black
1 green
1 white
A small amount of:
red, skin color

feathers

Five Fat Turkeys

118

Five Fat Turkeys

119

A PEANUT ON A RAILROAD TRACK   Toddler - 2nd Grade
(Origin Unknown)

A peanut sat on a railroad track
Its heart was all a flutter
A train came chugging down the track
Oops! Peanut Butter!

HERE COMES THE CHOO-CHOO TRAIN
(Action rhyme)

Here comes the choo-choo train
(elbows against sides, arms make forward circle)

Chugging down the track.
Now it's going forward...
Now it's going back.
(reverse circles)

Hear the bell a - ringing. Ding, dong, ding, dong
(hand above head making ringing motion)

Hear the whistle blow. Whoo - Whoo
(cup hands around mouth)

Chug, chug, chug
(arms circle slowly and pick up speed)

Chug, chug, chug
Everywhere it goes

Make a railroad track with a long strip of black felt. At the beginning of the song place the peanut in front of the train. At the end of the song remove the peanut and replace it with the peanut butter.

Color Suggestions	*Materials*
Engine - black	felt squares:
Box Car - green	1 black
Caboose - red	1 green
Peanut - tan	1 red
Jar - tan	A small amount of:
	tan

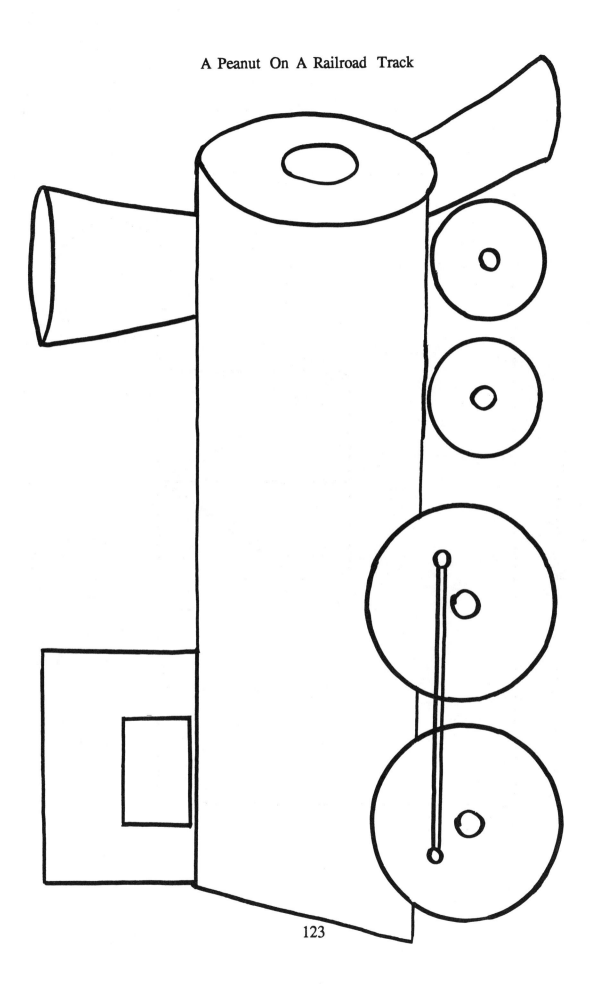

123

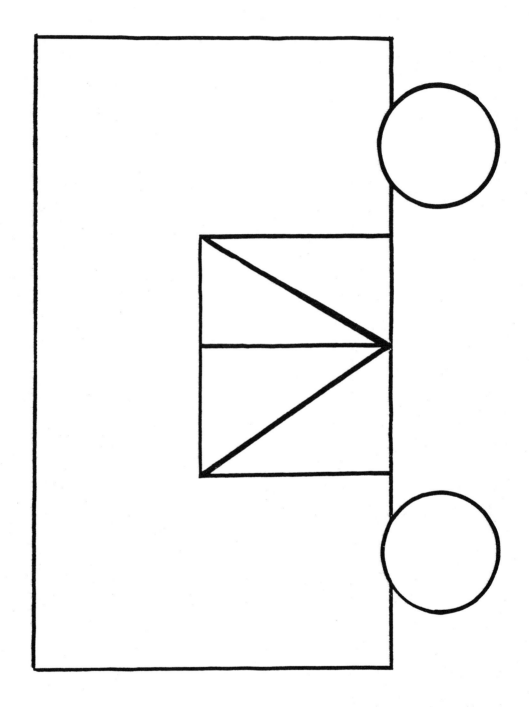

124

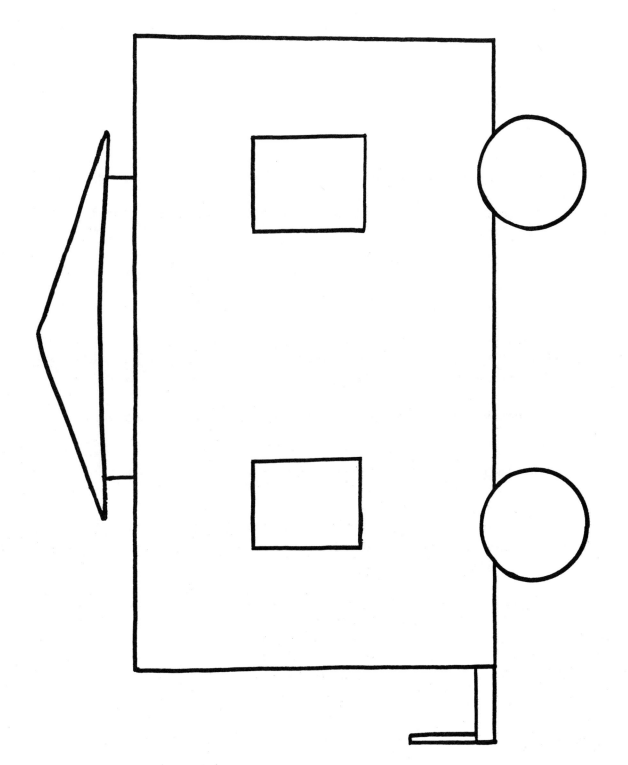

(An Irish tale)

One fine day a young man named Patrick O'Toole was out walking when he heard a tiny little sound coming from behind a nearby tree. He peeked behind the tree and he saw a wee little man dressed all in green. He was tapping with a tiny hammer, making shoes for the fairy folk. Patrick O'Toole grabbed hold of the leprechaun and said: "I caught myself a leprechaun!"

And the leprechaun said: "I'll thank you to let me go, sir, so I can get on with my work."

"Oh, no, you don't," said Patrick. "It's been told that when a leprechaun is caught, he has to show where his pot of gold is buried, and I demand that you show me!"

The leprechaun chuckled and said: "Oh, so it's my gold you're after, is it. Well, it seems I'll have to show you where it's hid."

So the leprechaun showed Patrick where to go to find the gold. They came to a field where lots of boliaun bushes were growing. The leprechaun pointed to one of them and said: "The pot of gold is under this bush. But you'll have to dig for it."

"I'll have to go and get a shovel," said Patrick. "But first I'm going to tie my red scarf on this bush so I'll know where to find it when I come back. Promise me you won't remove the scarf from this bush." (Patrick knew leprechauns always kept their word.)

"I will promise you that for sure," said the leprechaun. And then in a twinkling he was gone.

Patrick ran home as fast as he could to get the shovel. He was thinking all the while about how he could spend all that gold.

But when he got back to the field of boliauns he didn't want to believe what he saw. Every single boliaun bush in the field had a red scarf tied on it. He tried to dig where he thought the gold was but found none.

He became very downhearted and said: "That leprechaun got the best of me, that little trickster. But I'm going to carry my shovel with me wherever I go and when I catch that wee man again then I'll have my fortune for sure!"

So he carried his shovel with him for the rest of his days just in case he spied a leprechaun.

* Pronounced Bowl-Yawns

Directions

Make two boliaun fields by cutting out 3" x 18" tan felt pieces and gluing several bushes onto each. An easier option would be to use poster board backed with felt and paint or draw the boliaun bushes. If you do this, glue a small piece of velcro onto the first boliaun field so that Patrick's scarf will stick. To the second field glue several small pieces of red felt or ribbon (about 30).

Put the leprechaun in Patrick's hands when he is captured. When the leprechaun finally shows Patrick where the gold is, place the first boliaun field on the flannel board. Place the red scarf on the field before Patrick runs to get his shovel. At this point remove the leprechaun, Patrick, and the field from the flannel board.

When Patrick returns with his shovel put the field covered with ribbons on the flannel board.

Use the tree pattern from "Three Little Monkeys" (pp. 86-87).

Color Suggestions

Patrick - green cap, brown pants, white shirt, black shoes
Leprechaun - green clothes and shoes.

Materials

felt squares:
3 green
1 red
1 brown
A small amount of:
black, white, red

ribbon

The Field of Boliauns

scarf

Boliaun Bush

128

THREE LITTLE KITTENS

Three little kittens
They lost their mittens,
And they began to cry,
Oh, Mother dear,
We sadly fear
Our mittens we have lost.
What! Lost your mittens,
You naughty kittens!
Then you shall have no pie.
Mee-ow, mee-ow, mee-ow.
No, you shall have no pie.

The three little kittens
They found their mittens,
And they began to cry,
Oh, Mother dear,
See here, see here,
Our mittens we have found.
Put on your mittens,
You silly kittens,
And you shall have some pie.
Purr-r, purr-r, purr-r,
Oh, let us have some pie.

The three little kittens
Put on their mittens
And soon ate up the pie;
Oh, Mother dear,
We greatly fear
Our mittens we have soiled.
What! Soiled your mittens,
You naughty kittens!
Then they began to sigh,
Mee-ow, mee-ow, mee-ow,
Then they began to sigh.

The three little kittens
They washed their mittens,
And hung them out to dry;
Oh, Mother dear,
Do you not hear,
Our mittens we have washed.

129

What! Washed your mittens,
Then you're good kittens,
But I smell a rat close by.
Mee-ow, mee-ow,
Mee-ow,
We smell a rat
close by.

Directions

Make two clothesline poles with brown felt and glue a piece of string to them. Place the kittens on the flannel board without their mittens. Put the mittens on, take them off, and put them on the clothesline at the appropriate times. On the line "Oh, Mother dear, we sadly fear" place the mother cat on the board, holding the pie. Give the pie to the kittens on the line "And you shall have some pie."

Place the rat on the flannel board at the end of the poem.

Color Suggestions	*Materials*
Mother Cat - pink dress, blue apron	felt squares:
Kittens - white, grey, or orange	1 white
with stripes	1 grey
Clothes for kittens - yellow,	1 orange
pink, green	1 dark brown
Rat - dark brown	A small amount of:
Pie - tan	tan, pink, yellow
Mittens - red	red, blue, green
	A small piece of string

Three Little Kittens

131

THE SHOEMAKER AND THE ELVES   Preschool - 2nd Grade
(A Tale from Grimm)

There was once a shoemaker who made shoes and made them well. He worked very hard every day but he became poorer and poorer until he had nothing left but enough leather for one pair of shoes.

That night he cut out the leather for the last pair of shoes and went to bed.

When he got up the next morning he couldn't believe his eyes. There stood a pair of beautiful shoes all finished and perfectly made. The shoemaker did not know what to think but he set the shoes out for sale. Soon a man came and bought them and paid more than the usual price for them because they were such fine shoes. With this money the shoemaker was able to buy enough leather for two pairs of shoes.

Before he went to bed he cut the leather for the next day's shoemaking.

The next morning again he was surprised to see the shoes all made and ready to wear. He sold these for a good price and was able to buy even more leather.

Well, this went on night after night. Day after day more people came to buy the beautiful shoes and the shoemaker became rich.

Then one night, not long before Christmas, the shoemaker asked his wife, "How would it be if we stayed awake for a while? I would like to see who or what is being so good to us." "Yes," said his wife, "that I would like to know, too."

The shoemaker and his wife hid in a corner behind a curtain. And they waited there until at last, just at midnight, there came two cute little elves without a stitch of clothing to cover them. Quickly the little elves jumped onto the work bench and began making shoes. The shoemaker and his wife couldn't believe their eyes! The elves worked swiftly and skillfully with tiny flying fingers and didn't stop for a moment until all the shoes were finished. Then, in a twinkling, they leaped up and ran away.

The next morning the woman said, "I've been thinking that we should show our thanks to those two sweet little elves. They don't own a stitch of clothing. They're all bare and they must surely freeze. I want to make them each a little hat, a shirt, and breeches, and you can make them two little pairs of shoes, yes?" "Oh, yes I would very gladly do that," said the shoemaker.

The next night the man and his wife watched as the elves arrived ready to work. The elves looked around for the shoe leather and then they saw the row of little clothes lying on the workbench. First they wondered what the things were for and then they jumped for joy when they realized the clothes were for them. They dressed themselves in a twinkling and laughed and sang:

133

"Now we are jaunty gentlemen, Why should we ever work again?"

The elves were so happy! They danced and sang some more and clasped hands and merrily skipped out the door.

They never came back, but the shoemaker and his wife never forgot them and they lived happily and had good luck for the rest of their days.

Directions

Glue clothing and a face on both sides of the wife because she will need to face both directions at different times in the story.

Do not put the elves on the flannel board until they are seen by the shoemaker and his wife. At the end of the story dress them, sing the song to whatever tune you like, and remove them from the flannel board.

Color Suggestions	Materials
Clothes - red, green, brown yellow, pink	felt squares:
	1 red
Bench - brown	1 brown
Shoes - purple, red, green	1 green
	1 skin color
	A small amount of:
	pink, yellow, purple
	sequins for shoes

The Shoemaker and the Elves

Curtain

136

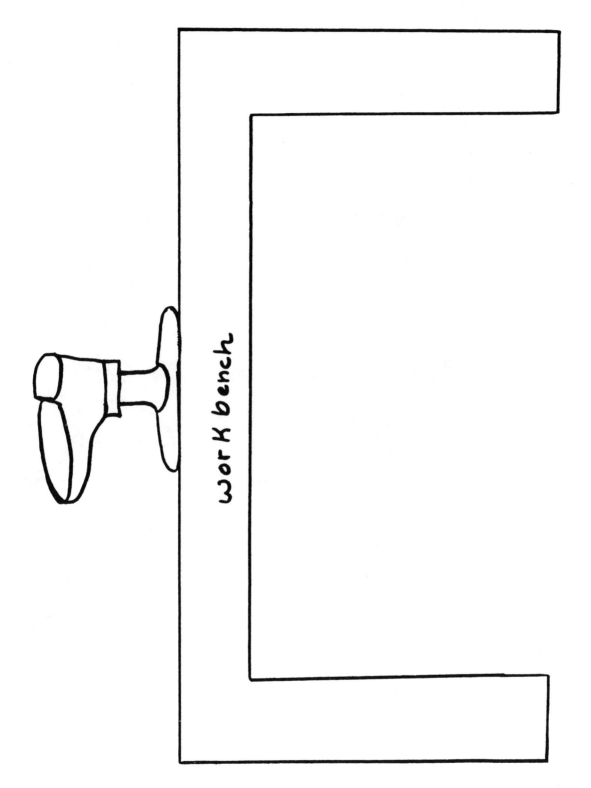

work bench

The Shoemaker and the Elves

138

(Author Unknown)

Five little froggies sat on the shore,
One went for a swim and then there were four.
Four little froggies looked out to sea,
One went swimming, and then there were three.
Three little froggies said, "What can we do?"
One jumped in the water and then there were two.
Two little froggies sat in the sun,
One swam off and then there was one.
One lonely froggie said, "This is no fun."
He dived into the water and then there was none.

Directions

Before starting the rhyme, place all the frogs beside the water. As you recite the rhyme have the frogs "jump" into the water one by one. Cut an oval of blue felt to represent the water. If your flannel board is blue, select a slightly different shade.

Materials

Felt squares:
2 green
1 blue

googly eyes

Five Little Froggies

140

Five Little Froggies

141

BIBLIOGRAPHY OF RESOURCES FOR STORYTIME PROGRAMMING

Baker, Augusta. *Storytelling: Art and Technique*. New York: Bowker, 1977.

Bauer, Caroline Feller. *Handbook for Storytellers*. Chicago: ALA, 1977.

Carlson, Bernice Wells. *Listen ! and Help Tell the Story*. New York: Abingdon Press, 1965.

Cole, Joanna. *The Eentsy Weentsy Spider: Fingerplay and Action Rhymes*. New York: Morrow Junior Books, 1991.

Glazer, Tom. *Eye Winker, Tom Tinker, Chin Chopper*. New York: Doubleday, 1973.

Lima, Carolyn. *A to Zoo: Subject Access to Children's Picture Books*. New York: Bowker, 1989.

MacDonald, Margaret Read. *Booksharing: 101 Programs to use with Preschoolers*. Hamden, Conn.: Shoe String Press, 1988.

MacDonald, Margaret Read. *The Storyteller's Sourcebook: A Subject, Title, and Motif Index to Folklore Collections for Children*. Detroit: Gale Research/Neal-Schuman, 1982.

Nichols, Judy. *Storytimes for Two-Year-Olds*. Chicago: ALA, 1987.

Oldfield, Margaret J. *Finger Puppets and Finger Plays*. Minneapolis: Creative Storytime, 1982.

Painter, William M. *Musical Story Hours: Using Music with Storytelling and Puppetry*. Hamden, Conn.: Shoe String Press, 1989.

Pellowski, Anne. *The Family Storytelling Handbook*. New York: Macmillan, 1987.

Pellowski, Anne. *The Story Vine: A Sourcebook of Unusual and Easy-to-Tell Stories from Around the World*. New York: Macmillan, 1984.

Peterson, Carolyn Sue. *Story Programs: A Source Book of Materials*. Metuchen, N.J.: Scarecrow, 1980.

Raffi. *The Raffi Singable Songbook*. New York: Crown, 1987.

Sawyer, Ruth. *The Way of the Storyteller*. New York: Viking, 1962.

Sierra, Judy. *Twice Upon a Time*. New York: H.W. Wilson, 1989.

Thompson, Richard. *Frog's Riddle and Other Draw-and-Tell Stories*. Toronto: Annick Press, 1990.

ABOUT THE AUTHOR

Diane Sherman Briggs is a children's librarian and storyteller at the Bethlehem Public Library in Delmar, New York. Previously an elementary school librarian, she holds an M.L.S. from the State University of New York at Albany.

The enthusiastic response of children to her flannel board stories has been the inspiration for this book.

Ms. Briggs lives in Delmar with her husband and five-year-old son.